Dedicated To:

Outdoor Writer Ed Erickson III and his son Kyle

**Who had a love for the outdoors and each other
like a father and son ought to have.**

(Their story is in Chapter 7)
(A Love Story From an Outdoor Man's Heart)

Phil. 1.6

God sure was good

John C. Walker

The Cover

The picture on the cover is that of Kyle Erickson and one of the nice bucks he shot.

As the dedication states, this book is dedicated to Kyle and his Dad. I guess a person would have to grow up in the woods of Upper Michigan to understand how a father and son can bond together out in the woods.

When you read the chapter on Kyle and his Dad maybe you will get a better insight into what I mean. I hope and pray that maybe someone out there will be able to love their son a little more, or a son love Dad a little more after reading this book.

As I have said over and over, "Life is so short, you want to make sure you enjoy every minute of it."

And as my dad always told me, "It seems that the older you get the faster the years seem to go by, so enjoy them while you can."

Index

D

Printed by:
A&J Printing
P.O. Box 518
Nixa, MO 65714

Published by: J.A.W.'S Publishing
2nd Printing.

Order from:
John A. Walker
530 Alger Ave.
Manistique, MI 49854
Phone: 906-341-2082
E-mail: jawspub@juno.com

Library of Congress Cataloging-In-Publication Data
Walker, John A.

ISBN 0-9639798-4-1

John A. Walker writes for:
Manistique Pioneer Tribune
212 Walnut St.
Manistique, MI 49854
Phone: 906-341-5200

These stories are written to show the humorous side of working as a Game Warden - living in Michigan U.P. They are not meant to offend anyone and are just the writers version of the stories as he heard or saw them happen. No names are used in the stories without prior approval.

Forwarned

This is Sgt. Walker's fifth book in a series of _Tales From A Game Warden._

Sgt. Walker's first book _(A Deer Gets Revenge)_ has become a best seller for self-published books. To date _A Deer Gets Revenge_ has sold almost 20,000 copies.

Five years ago, after retiring as a Michigan Conservation Officer, Sgt. Walker decided to put a number of the short stories he had written for his local newspaper the Manistique Pioneer Tribune into a book. Along with his first book, _A Deer Gets Revenge,_ Sgt. Walker has also self-published three other books.

The other three are, _A Bucket of Bones, From the Land Where BIG Fish Live,_ and _Luck, Skill, Stupidity._

Sgt. Walker wanted to start a scholarship fund at the church he attends to help youth attend Christian Colleges. In order to do this, he decided to write his books and place money from the books into this scholarship fund. To date they have almost $20,000 in certificates of deposit for the scholarship fund. By the time the 98-99 school year is over there will also have been over $10,000 in scholarships given out to students.

Sgt. Walker's books are humorous-family style tales told as his grandpa Thieler used to sit and tell his grandchildren stories back before the time of TV. They are written just like they were told around hunting camp or a campfire listening to grandpa once again.

This means that they will probably never be used in an English Literature class. That is unless they are used to tell the students how-not to use the English language.

When first talking about doing a book, Sgt. Walker was told to make sure that they were written in the same manner as the stories were told and later related in the Manistique Pioneer Tribune. You have to understand that this means the story structure may not fit into anything you have ever read before.

One time Sgt. Walker was asked by a BIG city newspaper, "Where did you attend college to learn to write in the style you do?" Sgt. Walker looked at the reporter and laughed, "I didn't, and we just talk like I write here in the

F

U.P. when telling stories."

People of all ages and walks of life love Sgt. Walker's books. People love everything from the humorous things that happen while working as a game warden, to the stories about growing up in the backwoods.

Each book has stories that try and teach family values and the importance of setting goals and enjoying life. One of the most interesting aspects of Sgt. Walker's books is the fact that people who he has never met feel they know him after reading his books. The phone calls and letters he receives from all over the country soon point out this to Sgt. Walker and his family.

If you like good, clean, humor and need to just be able to kick off your shoes once in a while and relax, you will love Sgt. Walker's books.

Dear Friend,

I guess there is no way that I deserve all the blessings I have received in my life. God has been so good to me. I listened to my Dad while growing up and ended up with the job I always wanted since my high school days. While in the army I met and married my wife and God blessed us with four wonderful children. Now we have six grandchildren. I could go on and on talking about the blessings of God, but there is something more important I would like to tell you about. While in the army a friend gave me a book titled The Greatest Story Ever Told. I read this book and it really got me thinking. Later I read the book called What would Jesus do? From these two books I started to wonder about Jesus dying on the cross once for all and I realized that all included me. After meeting my wife I asked the Lord to forgive my sins and come into my heart, but there was always a little question in my heart about being saved. A couple of years later I attended some special meetings being preached by a bear hunting friend of mine Evangelist Pete Rice. During these meetings I made sure about my salvation and have never had this doubt in my heart again.

Once I heard Brother Pete preach on John 3:16 For God so loved the world that he gave his only begotten son, that whosoever believeth in Him should not perish, but have everlasting life. At the end of his preaching six people walked the isle to get saved. One was a tough, old, trapper that I knew and it really impressed me. What does being saved mean? It simply means that one understands that Jesus came and died on the cross for our sins, that we understand we are a sinner, and we ask Jesus to come into our heart, forgive our sins, and be our Savior.

You can use what is called the Romans Road to help you with this. It is as easy as driving down a 2-track out in the woods. If you would take a Bible you would find these verses. Romans 3:23 AAll have sinned and come short of the glory of God. This means that all people have sinned and need to realize it. Romans 6:23 states, Athe wages of sin is death. This means if we do not ask forgiveness of God for our sins we will die with payment due for them. Corinthians 15:3 says, Christ died for our sins. This means payment has already been paid in full for our sins by Jesus death on the cross. Romans 6:23 tells us, the gift of God is eternal life through Jesus Christ our Lord. Everything that has to be done has been done, but for our part. Romans 10:13 tells us how, Whosoever shall call upon the name of the Lord shall be saved. This means all a person has to do is understand they are a sinner, that Jesus died on the cross for them, and ask Him to come into their heart and forgive their sins. Then you like so many before you will have everlasting life to look forward to.

I pray you will do this and someday I will see you in heaven and you can tell me about it.

The U.P.
Upper Michigan

Lake Superior

Ontonagon

Area I Worked
District IV
Area 7

Canada

COPPER
COUNTRY

ESCANABA

Manistique

Lake Huron

Wisconsin

Lake Michigan

Northern
Michigan

300 miles north of Milwaukee

300 Miles from Manistique to Lansing

First work
station

Down State

Lansing(capital)

Chapter 1
Conservation Officer's Stories
Upper Michigan Tales from a Game Warden's Perspective

Rocky

(Sgt. Walker has read this story at banquets around the state to people that could relate to this in their life. It has brought many a tear to a sportsman's eye as he read it)

Isn't it funny the way life goes? When you are young, the future seems so far away, but as the years go by reality seems to set in. I guess it is the same way with everything.

But as the years go by they just seem to move faster and faster. All those things you wanted to do, but never got around to. You now come to realize they will just never happen. Not that you are sorry for the way life has treated you, but it is just too short.

If you think our life passes by too fast, just stop and think a moment about your hunting buddy.

For some reason my wife never got jealous when I came home with blondish-red hair clinging to all my clothes. For some reason Wifee never figured she had anything to worry about. After all she knew good and well it only meant that my Golden, Rocky, and I were once again sitting next to each other as we went off on a hunting trip to the waterfowl marsh.

You have always heard the saying, "*The best things in life are free.*"
Well, I know this is true. A number of years back a friend of ours called and asked if we wanted a dog. It seemed that a party that trained hunting dogs had one all trained that needed a good home. I will have to say that it was one of my better moves in life the day Rocky came to live with us. This tale is dedicated to Rocky, who became a member of the family.

My Buddy, My Friend

Do you remember the title, "*When Time Stood Still?*" If not, I sure wish, I could have made it work a few years back. I guess there is nothing a hunter hates to see more then the years pass and his faithful hunting buddy getting older. You know it is coming, you know you can't stop it, but you still hate to see it happen.

I can remember the Falls only a few years back when the leaves started to turn and he just knew from some inbreed feeling that his time of the year was here. There was a look on his face and a prance in his steps, as he just knew we were off once again for the duck marsh.

Now, the look is still there. The prance is a little less and not so high off the ground. The desire and heart are still there, but the old bod is just not what it used to be. Try! He would kill himself trying to be the same and to please his hunting buddy. You.

As we walk into the marsh some of those log piles and treetops are just too high to bound over now. It used to be so easy and just watching his body clear these woodland obstacles was something to see. But now, he has to take a minute to see if he can get under them, or it just may be easier to take a little detour and just go around them. I just stand and wait till he catches up to me, because we are really not in that big a hurry any more and I know he used to have to stop and wait for me just a few years back when he had all that energy of youth.

We have had to forgo hunting some of those good old duck marshes where the mud is too deep now or the banks are just too high for him to climb out of the water over anymore. And to think that so few years back it was nothing to watch him conquer these marshes. In fact, I don't think I really care to hunt those places any more anyway. In fact, I'm not even sure waterfowl tastes as good as they used to back when it was so much fun to watch this bright, long haired, buddy of mine bound off the bank and swim across the marsh to bring the trophy back to his hunting buddy.

O' the look of pleasure on his face as he jumped out of the water, bounded up to you as you turned and ducked, because you knew what was coming, water-water everywhere. I have to wonder what kind of mind would jump into ice cold water, swim out after a duck or goose, crawl out of the mud onto the bank carrying his catch back to his master just to, while sitting there with eyes just sparkling, all for just a rub on the neck and a few "Good job, Rocky, way to go boy!"

I have to wonder if we humans would be better off if we would give our all for so little in return. To just be satisfied with an "Atta boy," once in a while.

Well, the last weekend of goose season the Lord was so good to us. We happened to come to this little pond. It has sand banks that are not too high, so I thought I would check it out. As I walked up, I at first thought there was nothing on it. But as I got closer to it a flock of geese took off and I fired one shot and two went down. I called Rocky back before he could go into retrieve the geese and walked back to the van. Here I got out my video camera and walked back to the pond. As Rocky went in to bring the geese back I stood there and made a few minutes of pictures of my buddy at work. It took him a while because you know a small goose is even bigger then it used to be now.

His heart is still as big as ever, but when he gets out of the water you really don't have to duck anymore. It seems the trailer does not move as good as it used to and the water does not soak you like it did a few years back. But, when he picks up his goose, because it has never been me that made this all work out, but him, and heads back to the van to jump in with his days work, I shut off the camera and wish I were not making memories like I know I am.

Just maybe when that day comes, as we all know it will, and I go to that perfect hunting place in the sky, I will be sitting at the edge of a duck marsh and feel a wet cold nose trying to get between my arm and body, so I can give a big, not old any more wet head, a hug. Because I have always been taught that heaven is a perfect place and we all know it could not be a perfect place if it did not have our faithful hunting dog there with us now could it?

You know it's hard to make this gadget work with tears in your eyes.

Rocky & A Little Buddy

Chapter 2
Conservation Officer's Stories
Upper Michigan Tales from a Game Warden's
Perspective

The True Skills of Being A Hunter

For some reason, hunters out there seem to think that just because a person becomes a game warden they have almost super natural powers when it comes to hunting and fishing. If only the truth was known about their true skill and ability when it came to having a successful hunting season! The following may just help you have a better understanding of how things really happen out in the woods.

I guess there has to be at least a zillion *Exspurt* deer hunters out there. On top of this there has to be more than a zillion *can't miss* items for the hunter to use to make sure that he gets the really big buck. If all this confuses us did you ever wonder what the deer must think?

One time I did a story about the zillions of fishing lures for anything and everything and all of them guaranteed to catch fish. We used to laugh about this, but now deer hunters are in the same boat. What to use where, how, and when? Before the rut, during the rut, after the rut, a doe in heat, a doe not in heat, smoke poles, apple blocks, grunts, horns to rattle, and on and on. If they all work a small percentage of what they claim they do, deer would soon be on the endangered list. But instead maybe normal hunters are.

I thought I would take this chapter and tell a few tales about the biggest bucks I ever bagged. Now not the biggest I have observed in my travels, but these were nice enough to make it to the basketball backboard on the front of my garage.

A Helping Hand

This started out being one of those years when things just did not seem to want to fall into place. It was super cold with a lot of snow. Where I was hunting there were a lot of deer moving around, but not when I was there to see them. (I was still working during this time.) I guess there is nothing worse than knowing there is a buck in the area and never seeing one. But I almost always sit in the same spot during the whole season.

I had a nice warm blind that is open to the weather, but built to protect you from the wind. I had a bait pile out by an old stump in front of the blind and beyond the bait pile the terrain went down into a creek bottom. Behind me were a lot of oak ridges that the deer would go into at night to eat. Tons of deer signs, but no bucks.

The only other thing I ever did was to make a few scrapes and rubs of my own. I figured if the bucks were too lazy to make any, I would help them out. Whether it ever fooled the deer, I may never know, but it sure impressed a crew of Trolls from down state when they saw them all over the place. That is until I explained to them that I had made them with an old stick.

The other thing that made this a rather interesting year is the fact that there was a crew cutting on Forest Service land right across the creek from me. On these cold, snow covered days it sounded like they were standing right in front of my blind. You could hear them arrive right after daylight in the morning, haul their gear out of the trucks, crank up their power saws and go to work. Most of the crews would cut till around 3:30 or 4:00 before they called it a day. Then it would give me a little more then an hour for things to quiet down and the deer to start moving. A few did, a doe and her fawns every night, but no bucks.

By now it was getting late in the rifle season and I had a couple of days off for the Thanksgiving Holidays. My plans were to go in with a buddy and remove my blind so I could spend the last few days hunting an area with a little peace and quiet. We went into the area of my blind and before we took it down we scouted the area a little while. Up on the top of the ridge behind the bait pile we found the tracks of a big deer. Following these tracks just a little way we found a big buck scrape. Then later where he went down into the creek bottom. Again proof that there was a nice buck in the area, so should I remove my blind? I figured being a holiday period that the pulp cutters would surely take a few days off, this should give me a couple of nice quiet days to hunt the creek bottom from my blind without anyone making more noise then a person should have to listen to from their blind! Right? Wrong!

I went into my blind well before daylight to let things quiet down. I was sitting there with my little heater going just enjoying life as things started to lighten up. About the time you could see really good looking through the trees my whole plan fell apart! Across the creek I heard a couple of pickups come into the cutting and sure enough the crew was going to work on Thanksgiving. In fact they worked on the Friday after Thanksgiving. So needless to say I was still without a buck going into the last couple of days of season.

I had one more evening to hunt, so figured I may as well go out and sit. Sure enough the crew was cutting across the creek. It was so still on this day you could hear everything they were doing. About 3:30 I heard a couple of trucks pull out of the area, but there was still someone over there hard at work and it sure sounded like he was going to work till dark. But there was nothing I could do.

All of a sudden I heard a loud yell from across the creek and the sound of a big tree going down. Right on the cutter's pickup! How did I know this? I could hear him talking to himself about what had taken place like he was standing right in front of my blind. He was not a happy pulp cutter to say the least. He used some words that would have got me in bad trouble if I had used around my Mommie.

Then I heard the chain saw start up and run a while, then go off. I could then hear him as he removed the tree parts he had just cut from his truck. The saw would start up again and he would go through the process again. He must have finally got it all off his truck because I heard items hitting the back of the truck as the chain saw and the rest of his equipment was tossed into the truck. The truck then started up and he must have held it to the floor all the way out to the main road. Needless to say he was mad!

I sat there figuring that it was another wasted day after all that noise when all of a sudden I saw movement on top of the ridge to the right of my apple pile, between me and the area where the cutter had just left after making enough noise to wake up the dead. It was a big deer, just maybe . . . Out it stepped and it was a big deer all of her! Just a huge doe walking down toward, my bait pile, then turning up and going over the ridge down into the creek bottom. Wait, but there comes another deer right behind her. As it stepped out of the trees, I saw it was a really nice buck.

Now I have areas picked out where I have already made plans to shoot at any buck as he walks through the area. This buck has his head down near the ground and is coming down the ridge right toward me! I figured that he is never going to come all the way into the open area by the bait pile, so I better take a shot the first chance I get. I pulled up and aimed for the front of his chest as he angled just a little away from me. Wham! Down he went and never so much as a twitch.

I waited a minute before I got out of my blind and walked up to the buck. He was a nice nine pointer. I was totally amazed at how quick he went down after shooting at the chest area, but who am I to complain. The funny thing is, there is no doubt in my mind that if the logger had not dropped that tree on his truck and made all the noise he did, this buck would never have moved out of the creek bottom as early as he did. If it had been fifteen-twenty minutes later, it would have been too close to dark to shoot this buck through the trees.

See all the skill that was involved! But that is not the best part. I took the deer home and a couple of days later I was going to skin it and cut it up. I started at the neck and pulled the hide down and as I went by the area of the chest I thought, "This is funny there is no bullet hole anywhere in the chest area." I finished skinning the deer and from where I started at the neck to its tail there was no sign of a bullet hitting this buck. Now I had to find out just what happened.

I went up on the neck and started to remove the hide going up near the antlers. Finally about two inches below the antlers I found where I had hit this buck. I could say I planned to hit him here all the time because I didn't want to ruin any meat. Or, why when you're as good a shot as I am, why shoot at the wide area of the chest on a deer, when you can hit him in the back of the neck as he comes down a ridge. Or could it be that I almost missed this nice buck and was just lucky?

It's All In The Timing

I have to wonder if this tale should really have been in my book titled *Luck, Skill, or Stupidity!*.

If you know anything about me, you know that I spend just about all the time I can get away with from the middle of September till the middle of December out in the woods. I love it out there. Plus, I have always felt that the key to being a successful deer hunter was to spend enough time learning and scouting out an area. Take time to learn the deer's habits and to look the area where you are going to hunt over good. Look for scrapes and rubs; spend some evenings to learn where and when the deer are moving. I do all this.

Then I spend a lot of time trying to figure out just where and how to place my deer blind. Even after doing all this I may end up shifting or moving it a little till I feel I have it just right. On the pre-hunt this year things were no different. I still had my old stand-by blind where I usually sit 90% of the time during deer season. But, I wanted to find a place where just maybe I could get one of those *first thing in the morning bucks.* I have yet to ever get a buck first thing opening morning so this year I worked on it. 'Cause I've got them at the noon buffet, the evening supper, or just walking around in the woods when I got tired of sitting, but I have never got one of those breakfast deer. But as I said this year I had a plan!

Everything looked great where I planned to sit. We had already observed a buck at this blind during bow season. So just maybe if I sat there opening morning I would get a first, just maybe!

Opening morning we rolled out at 5:00am (That's in the morning way before daylight and before normal people are even thinking of getting up.) We fixed some toast and hot chocolate for breakfast. That good old toast burned over an open gas flame washed down with a couple of cups of rich hot chocolate, life couldn't get any better. My boy headed off to his blind, while I filled my thermos with coffee and headed for mine.

Into the blind well before daylight. Set things up, with a sleeping bag over my legs, my little heater under my chair to keep me warm, what more could a guy ask for. Now to just sit and wait for daylight.

Now, you must take a minute to understand that I do everything while hunting according to a pre-made plan. I get to the blind at a set time, have to have everything ready and quite at a certain time, Can only have my cup of coffee at a certain time, each hour on the hour. First a cup at 8:00, second one at 9:00, third at 10:00, etc. Then my plans were to pull out at 11:00 right on the dot to head back to meet up with my boy at noon. I always felt that the key to everything is to have a plan and stick to your plan.

It was a quiet morning in the area where I was hunting; in fact it was so quiet that I never saw a thing. But, truly a nice morning as daylight approached over the snow-covered woods. 8:00 rolled around as I sat in my blind and as my game plan called for I had my first cup of coffee. I never saw another hunter or any deer as 9:00 rolled around and it was coffee time again. This on top of my first cup of coffee and my two cups of hot chocolate and toast. Still really quiet as 10:00 rolled around as I was reading from a book I had brought along. Coffee time, then only about an hour till it would be time to head out to meet the boy.

Now when I say that my plans are to sit till 11:00, I mean I try to sit till 11:00 on the dot before I pull up and head out. The plans are to sit until 11:00, collect my gear, and head back to the trailer. I have always been this way when out hunting.

On this opening morning the wind was blowing at least a zillion miles an hour through the pine trees I was sitting in. My little portable blind that I had made up, to meet all the new requirements placed on hunting blinds by the DNR, started to remind me of the Wright Brother's first airplane. My only hope to keep from getting blown away was that I had tied my new, lightweight, portable blind to a small pine tree with an environmentally friendly rope, to keep it from getting airborne.

As the 10:00 hour and my third cup of coffee, on top of two cups of hot cocoa, came and left, while now just sitting there waiting for 11:00 and departure time to roll around, I started to realize something! I think you could call it the first telltale signs of kidney failure! No Problem! It was now almost 10:30, so I would just not move around too much and sit it out. At about 10:40 I noticed a remarkable phenomenon that all true sportsmen face once in a while. As I looked out through the trees, as the wind blew the trees back and forth, and my deer blind tied to this small pine tree with my environmentally friendly rope went back and forth with the trees, I started to observe whitecaps in my eyeballs that told me that the best hunting plans sometimes just may be in trouble and call for some major changes! Or else!

At 10:45 it was, don't move around at all! In fact don't even breathe too deep! And just maybe you will make it till 11:00! At 10:50 it came to a major change in my plans right now! Out the front of the blind went my sleeping bag, followed by my thermos, (minus three cups of coffee), the heater, and the bag with the rest of my hunting gear! Out of the blind I went planning to grab my gear and make a beeline for the road. But then the second thing all true deer hunters are aware of took place!

When you have been sitting in one spot as long as I had been, out in the cold not moving around, when you first start moving again, you have a real problem. The problem is that there is no way you are ever going to make it out to the road before . . . So off he goes about twenty feet from the blind. There he stands and as he looks up he observes this deer coming right at him! It then throws up its tail when it sees him and bounds off through the trees. See! It would have walked right by the blind if I had been able to sit till 11:00 as I had planned to do. But! As he looks back on the tracks, where the doe that had just run off came from, along comes this second deer right on her track with its nose right down on the ground! And here he stands without a gun!

Without his gun, for it is twenty feet back of him still in the deer blind! He is in serious trouble. Off he runs for the deer blind and his gun, grabs the gun, and jumps to the right side of the blind to look down the runway the buck was on! Nothing! It's gone! Not a deer in sight! Back across the front of the blind he jumps to look off the left side of the blind. There it is! Standing right behind the blind about ten feet away, behind a little spruce tree trying to hide from this big dummy in the bright orange suit that was running back and forth in the woods. In fact he was so close the hunter could not find him in the scope, so he just points the gun at the buck and pulls the trigger.

See hunting is a true science. So grab your thermos and go for it. By the way, it was a nice 7-point buck.

Some Things Are Just Meant To Be

There are always those days that when they first start out they seem to go from bad to worse. There are hunting seasons that fall into this same category. Nothing seems to go right.

I had a great looking spot I was hunting this season. There were a lot of deer signs in the area and some trappers had observed a nice 8-point buck near my blind. I was still working at this time so it meant hunting in between working hours. I saw a good number of deer the first couple of days but never a buck. I finally got a day off and planned to spend all day out at my blind.

I got there early in the morning well before daylight and got all set up. There was a buddy of my boys hunting his blind on this day. (My boy was off at college) I heard a shot up the creek bottom right after daylight and watched a couple of deer move in and out of the opening where my bait pile was. It was just getting into prime hunting time when I heard this crazy noise of metal on metal coming in behind me! At first I could not figure out what it was as it kept getting closer and closer, but finally figured it must be my buddy from the other blind coming in to get me. Just maybe that shot I had heard earlier in the morning had been Billy.

Here I sat and waited till a party came around the trees to the front of my blind. Here comes this guy dragging a folding chair right up to my blind! As I leaned forward and stuck my head out he said, "O' you're here!" I thought he had to be a Troll 'cause if he had looked down he would have saw fresh tracks in the snow, even if there was no vehicle parked out on the two-track. It appears he had planned to sit at my blind when he failed to see a car parked where I always park. The only problem is that my blind is only open at the top half of the front of the blind. You have to step over a three-foot board to get into it. This *hunter?* was too fat and out of shape to step into the blind so he was dragging a metal chair to sit on near my blind. But, this morning was shot for the deer had moved out when the folding chair rattled its way in. Nothing else today.

I finally got another chance when I could get into the blind and it was a nice looking evening. The deer were really working the area and just maybe. I sat here for a couple hours and had one doe and a fawn come in for a snack, but nothing else. I must have been sitting there in never, never land when all of a sudden, wham! Someone shot right in front of my blind! Right between it and the creek! I peeled myself off the roof of the blind where I had splattered when the shot went off right out in front of my blind.

 As I sat there, I got thinking. I had not observed any deer in a while, so I wonder what the shot was about? I crawled out of my blind and started to walk toward the creek. About the time I hit the top of the hill I saw this hunter coming toward me. I walked up to him and looked beyond him and saw the pat he had shot laying on the ground. It is not good to shoot pats out of season right in front of a Game Warden=s deer blind. Another day shot!

But! I did have all day Thanksgiving Off! So off I went to my deer blind to try once again. Fresh snow on the ground-it should be a great day. During this time of season things really slow down up in this area after most first week hunters have returned home. I was sitting in my blind reading a book, when once again, only this time right behind me, out where the two-tracks intersect, whamm! Only this time was even louder for it was definitely a deer rifle. I then heard a car pull out a few minutes later.

Once again I figured just maybe I should see what they shot. I walked out to the road and back tracked their vehicle a little way up over a hill. Here I saw where they had stopped, backed up a little way, and I then saw where someone had got out of the passenger side of the vehicle and walked back in the woods. I followed this one set of tracks back to the area of some small poplar trees and here I saw blood on the snow and what was left of a partridge lying on the ground. I looked around and as I was walking back out to the road I found a rifle shell that had been ejected laying on top the fresh snow.

I went over the hill, got into my car, and started to follow the tracks of the vehicle that had shot the pat. I followed them out to a main gravel road, (remember there was fresh snow on the ground), where they took a right turn. I then followed them down this road to a dead end road they turned onto. I went down this road and stopped their vehicle coming back out. I checked the hunters out and found the same caliber gun, matching the shell I had found near where the pat was shot. I seized the gun and wrote the party a ticket for shooting a pat out of season. (The state police crime lab later matched the empty casing to the firearm I had seized.) I often wondered how these two men felt after they pull up, shoot a pat out of season with a deer rifle, just to kill it 'cause it was blown all to pieces, then drove the rest of the way over the hill and see a Game Warden's marked patrol car parked right off the road.

But I was still getting skunked as far as deer season went. But the way this season was going what more could happen? I finally had another afternoon to go out and sit in my blind. There was a lot of snow on the ground and it was just great being out there. About an hour before dark a couple of deer moved into the opening. All of a sudden I saw a really big deer through the trees on the top of the little ridge behind my bait pile. It would take a few steps and stop, take a few more steps and stop, and it was getting on toward dark. It finally moved in behind the bait pile near a clump of maple trees and stopped. You tell me how a big deer can stop right behind an eight-inch tree; hide its whole body, with only one eyeball looking around the tree at you! And stands there until its too dark to see if its a doe or a buck! O'well at least I saw some deer.

On the next night I got into the blind at the last minute. I would only have a little more then an hour to sit, but you never can tell the way this season has been. A short time after I got settled in my blind, just when the deer should start moving, all of a sudden it sounded like the school bus had let out down in the creek bottom. O'man what next! All I could hear were a number of guys over in the creek bottom yelling at each other. I finally figured it must be some of my *buddies?* That knew where I hunted trying to get my goat. It was working!

It finally quieted down and right than I saw movement through the trees right where I had seen the big deer the night before coming up from the creek. I waited and waited till finally a nice buck stepped over a dead fall into the opening. I waited for one of my shooting spots, aimed right behind his front shoulders just like the books says, and when he took another step let him have it! Down he went and never moved. It was a nice 8-point buck dropped with a perfect neck shot. I figured it must not really matter where you hit them, just so you hit them where they're living, right?

Chapter 3
Conservation Officer's Stories
Upper Michigan Tales from a Game Warden's
Perspective
Things To Ponder

Going through life can sure be an interesting project; the only problem is that about the time you get it figured out you are at the wrong end. This and a lot of other little brain twisters make up this chapter. Ideas and thought that just came along while you were sitting somewhere letting your mind wander. Some may make sense, while others just seemed interesting at the time they flew by.

Maybe you have been there and have a few of your own, but here are some of mine.

1- Going through life can sure be an interesting project, the only problem is that just about the time you think you have it figured out you're at the wrong end.

2- It is better to always set a high goal and shoot a little under it, then to set no goal at all and hit it.

3- Always try a little better than your best.

4- The true test of being an adult is admitting that there is something out there everyday that you can learn from.

5- Never quit wanting to learn.

6- Life is just to short for us having fun, so take time out to stop and smell and enjoy the flowers. (This is nothing new, but I had to remind my children about this when they were trying to do too much all at once.)

7- Learn to enjoy all those things God placed out there for us that are free to enjoy.

8- Always! Always! Always treat others just as you would like to be treated if you were in the same place under the same conditions. (I always told this to new officers that were just starting out.)

9- There are no "dumb" kids out there, there are just those that never learned to study and apply themselves, then do their best at the project they were working on.

10- Treat all your kids the same no matter how many the Good Lord may have given you.

11- Some of the greatest lessons that can be learned come from those that are truly handicapped living around us.

12- If you ever achieve perfection there would just be nothing to accomplish anymore. (I think of this when I find mistakes in my books that really bug me to the fact we missed them.)

13- A wife must have the patience of Job, the Wisdom of Solomon, the foresight of an old testament Prophet to live for years with a man that likes his hunting and fishing.

14- Always remember that you love your wife, you only like to hunt and fish.

15- To destroy is easy, to ruin sometimes simple, but it's a real project to build something that will last.

16- True friends are those that are willing to help you in the time of need when there is nothing to be gained for them from doing it.

17- Why build your reputation all year long, than throw it away while on a single hunting or fishing trip.

18- Remember when out in the woods where nobody is watching, your kids tend to see the real you come to the surface.

19- How come the obvious truly escapes our attention so many times?

20- Why do we have to lose something before we realize how important it was to us?

21- Why is it so hard for so many people to say to someone how they feel about them, before they look at them for the last time at the funeral home?

22- Why do people always try to sell us old retired people something with a lifetime guarantee?

23- Did you ever stop and think of all you learned from people that in the eyes of today's *Exspurts* did not know anything and should never have been teaching you?

24- Remember, everybody is a teacher of some kind, either teaching the youth around them the good or the bad things of life.

25- How come a house that you could live in all your life is so hard to purchase and you have to place so much money down, but a car that can cost twice as much and not last a small percentage of what the house will, you can walk in sign a paper and drive out in it? Is life backwards sometimes?

26- Why is a lie no longer a lie, and someone who always tells the truth is considered old fashioned?

27- If you go ahead and do something you want to do, knowing that after you do it there will be some results from your actions you won't like, don't complain about it later.

28- If you ask someone a question, knowing the answer will not be what you want to hear even before you ask the question, don't be surprised or upset about it.

29- Remember before you make some of those big steps in life; there is a lot of wisdom in some of those old gray heads around you, which have walked down this same path before you.

30- Remember that some things never change, they just get lost in all the hustle and bustle of this day and age and you have to just look harder to see them.

31- Remember what impressed wifee when you were dating her, will be what keeps the honeymoon going all your years together.

32- Do the unexpected to the unsuspecting, be a help to someone else.

An endangered-threatened specie I like to look for

My hunting buddy with dad's deer, see the smile?

Chapter 4

Conservation Officer's Stories

Upper Michigan Tales from a Game Warden's
Perspective

Twains

Every once in a while a story comes along that when you first hear it you are sure nothing like that could ever happen. There just are not people in this world that would put themselves in a situation where something like the tales told below could ever take place. I heard this tale from a number of people and even saw the results of what took place (Wifee's trailer) out at the scene. Now, remember this is the story as it was told to me.

The Troll Twain

Well, it seems that there were these people from below the bridge that decided they were going to become deer hunters. They have seen all these reports about being a Yooper deer hunter, watched all those outdoor programs, and just figured there's nothing to this, anybody could become a deer hunter.

Off they went for the Great North Woods with all their gear, the wifee's nice new house trailer to use as their deer camp, with visions of grandeur in their eyes. After all they had some orange clothes, a hunting license, and a road map, so this must make them a deer hunter, right?

They had no trouble finding the U.P. and just headed west on US-2. Right off they saw that there was nothing to this deer hunting business! Why they even had a crosswalk marked for deer along US-2, just like they had for people down in the city where they lived. And to make it even better they had them marked where just the bucks could cross. Hunters had it made up here.

They made it about eighty-five miles west of the bridge, when one of the guys, the map reader, must have figured they had to be in "The Big Buck Country." "Lets turn off here," was heard from the navigator. (Take my word for it; this has to be the first crew of hunters since the beginning of time that decided to turn off on this road in this area for their hunt. Maybe they figured there is no way we can get lost because we can watch for the airport light.) They went down this gravel road, everyone knows deer live off gravel roads, take a left on the first two-track. Man! This has to be deer country! (No! It's an old closed down dump, but remember these are Trolls on their first adventure to get the big one.)

Down to the end of the road, or should I say the normal people's end of the road. But, there is this two-track sand road that leads even farther back into the real heart of the big buck country. Just maybe we are going to be back where not even *"Wagon Train"* had traveled before, or just maybe they were the last ones through here! But as life goes, all good things must come to an end and so did this two-track sand road! I mean right now! With no place to turn wifee's twenty-five foot trailer around. They were getting their first lesson in travel in the U.P. that was not covered in all those Troll Land outdoor shows.

Here they, (by the way I forgot to tell you that this all was taking place in the middle of the night because we all know that Troll's like to travel into paradise under the cover of darkness), were trying to turn the trailer with the vehicle attached around. They got stuck, then they got really stuck, then things got even worse. Finally they got their vehicle turned around and the trailer was so hung up there was no way they could get it to move. They then put their heads together, if there is anything more dangerous then teenagers thinking something out, it must be a herd of Trolls, and thought they would just head out and get a motel room for what was left of the night and pick up the trailer in the morning. After all it would be a lot easier in the daylight, right? Wrong!

Do you have any idea how many two-track roads there are off all the gravel roads in the U.P.? They could not remember where they had turned off or where wifee's trailer could be. Now being true Trolls they knew that if you have any problems you always ask the policeman on the corner. So off they went to find a policeman. When they did find one they had come up with a great tale because no Troll ever wanted a Yooper to think they may not be too bright from living so long down below that big bridge. So they told the officer they had left their trailer along the road when they had trouble with it and went back this morning and it was gone. They didn't lie. It was a road, well almost a road.

This wise officer sitting there must have known that there was more to the story so he told them, "Now, tell me what really happened." So our Trolls finally told them how they had come north deer hunting, turned off on a gravel road, then on a two-track, had got stuck with their trailer, and now for the life of them could not figure out where they were last night in the dark or where the trailer was. The officer asks them what time all this took place? He was told, "It must have been right around midnight when we got the trailer hung up and so stuck, that we figured we may as well leave it there for the rest of the night. We then went to get a motel room to return at daylight for our trailer."

The police officer's famous words, that will stick in the minds of these Trolls forever went something like this, "It must have been fifteen-twenty minutes after you left that the train came through." The moral of the story is that it is not good to get wifee's camper trailer hung up on the railroad tracks and just leave it there for the train to get off! As our hubby Troll deer hunter walked out the door at the post saying over and over, "WhatamIgoingtotellthewifee--WhatamIgoing.."

Stupidity Strikes Again!

If you live in the U.P. you are well aware that one of the biggest activities in the winter is snowmobiling. For some reason there is a certain percentage of these crews that figures the only way you can enjoy this sport is to travel at 100 miles an hour from bar to bar. This must have been what took place on this day.

It seems that there were about eight snowmobilers that had been out for a while filling themselves with a little anti-freeze at each stop they made. I have no way of knowing how many times they did this before they got to their last stop, but it must have been quiet a few.

At the last bar they stopped at they all parked their snowmachines in the same area and went into the bar. They spent their usual time in the bar and then decided to continue on their travels. Out they came but they couldn't find their snowmachines!

They knew where they had left them, the tracks were right there in the show showing how they had come into the bar, Yes, this is where they were. But, no machines in sight now. Just a minute there is another set of tracks right where our machines were. Yup, could those tracks have something to do with the missing snow machines?

As they checked things out sure enough the other set of tracks would sure enough explain where their snowmachines went.

You see it seems that our mental giants had come along to the bar and parked all eight of their snowmachines in the same spot. Right in the middle of the railroad tracks!

Chapter 5

Conservation Officer's Stories
Upper Michigan Tales from a Game Warden's Perspective

Backwoods (Yooper's) Vehicles

I guess one of the biggest bummers of a game warden retiring is the fact he has to give up all his toys. That and the fact that he has to turn in his credit card and start buying his own gas for his travels through the backwoods.

Now, when I started out with the state, you drove your own car and were paid so much a month for its use. Later they started assigning us patrol cars that had basically the same specks as the Michigan State Police patrol vehicles. It was a whole lot of years later that someone finally convinced the powers in being that a 4x4 pickup was what we really needed. But, it was something where those patrol cars would go.

One time I was way back *in the middle of no-where* on a 2-track road. To get where I was we had to travel through some mud holes that were unreal. This and the fact there where some rutty, muddy hills getting back into the area, we wanted to work. But, as the old saying goes, *"It is hard to get stuck at 60 miles an hour!"* That and the fact, *"You are never stuck till you stop!"* So in other words, floor it! and keep on going.

As we were working back in this area off Lake Superior, we came across some bear hunters. As we were checking them out one of the hunters said, "I didn't think we were going to make it through those holes getting back here!" Here they were with a big wheeled, 4x4 Chevy pickup. This truck had a special suspension, two four-barrel carbs on it, and all the other toys a guy puts on his truck. As he made this statement here we stood next to our little patrol car, a 440-Plymouth sedan with just normal everyday tires on it and no extras, and we had come through all those same mud holes he had worried about traveling through. I guess it's just mind over matter, if you are going fast enough all the mud in the world will not matter!

After I turned my 4x4 patrol pickup in, I just had to get a 4x4 of my own. I mean you cannot be a normal Yooper if you don't have one. This first tale kind of lets you know what I hoped for.

A Yooper's Backwoods Vehicle

And There She Was!

Well, while traveling down through Missouri I almost went off the deeeeep end. Now, make sure none of you tell my wifee about this, because I almost fell in love, again. But I fought it off and returned home with the wifee and family all in one piece.

Now, you sportsmen out there that like to hunt and fish will know what I am talking about. Here I was just north of Springfield, Missouri traveling along with my wifee and daughter minding my own business when I looked off to the left and there she stood! There was no way you could miss her the way she was built! I had been dreaming for years and looking all over the country for someone just like her and now there she stood. I quickly switched lanes, on the four-lane. Thank goodness there was a stop light right there so I could make a left and turn across the other lanes without getting us all killed. I drove through a Hardee's right up to her for a better look.

Even up close she was all I ever expected her to be. From the ground up she was something to behold. I got out to take an even closer look. A dream comes true! Anything and everything a normal, red blooded, Yooper, outdoorsman could ever want right before my eyes. In fact she was so good looking my daughter even got out to look at her too. As I stood there looking, with my mouth maybe hanging open a little, with just maybe a little drool running out, along came this party to point out her finer points to me. I really did not have to be sold on her, but let him try.

She was white from the top of her roof, down to the brand-new four tires she stood on. Not a mark on her anywhere! In the inside were cloth seats, so you would not freeze up here in the North Country during the winter months. All the gauges I wanted. Four wheel drive with a bed liner in the back. Maaaan! But, the best was yet to come. From the automatic transmission I wanted, too under the hood, where sat the very engine I always dreamed of. It was a 6.2 turbo-diesel with a personally autographed valve cover from Mr. Goodwrench just for me. My heart just fluttered. It had to be love at first sight!

The party pointing out her finer points to me tried to tell me about some other ones besides her, but it was hopeless. He showed me one without her extended cab, but no way! In fact I pointed out to him that without it wifee would have to hold Rocky on her lap when we were out duck hunting after he got all wet. No! There was no way he could ever show me anything else. I was hooked.

I took wifee to her brothers, then her brother and I returned for one more look. My feelings had not changed even the little while we were apart. I walked around her a few more times showing her off to wifee's brother. He saw right away why I felt like I did. But, his wife had warned him even before he left the house that this was mine; so don't even think about it! Some wives are just more understanding than others.

I asked the guy there, "If I give you wifee's car what are my chances of getting her?" He figured it all out and I thought and fought it over in my mind. How could I just walk away from her after all this time of trying to find someone just like her? But, after thinking it all over and hurt as it may, I finally figured it may be best to just turn my back on her, and walk away. I did not dare look back even for a final glance.

But, I still sit here thinking of her, pure white, from bumper to bumper, brand new oversize tires, an extended cab with a beautiful interior, plus, that personally autographed 6.2 Turbo-diesel. Would I ever meet someone like her again? At my age it could be bad news to leave a true love, hoping to meet her again someday, but I did. It may be a good thing nobody ever wrote a song, "I Left My Heart in Springfield, Missouri."

Next To Nothing!

Up above is what I would have liked to buy, but then the real world always seems to set in. I always tell my teenage daughter, "I would really buy it, except for one little thing, money!" It seems that this is always the little thing that keeps us humble.

So I looked around for one I could afford and live with. Now, I just had to have a 4x4 pickup or else why get anything at all. In my travels I finally found one that looked like maybe I could afford to buy it. It was at the Chevy garage so I was on the right track. I went in and talked to a salesman. He told me what they wanted for it and I offered him half as much. He told me, "The drive train is worth more then that if we sold it for junk." I ask him what the drive train was worth and ended up buying it for this amount.

I don't mean to say my new, 4x4-hunting truck was junk, but he's the one that brought it up. I fell in love with it right off, seeing it was a Luv pickup. It had some qualities all its own seeing it had been rolled over once or twice. The doors were rather neat too. When you opened them, they dropped down about four inches, so to close them you had to pull up as hard as you could at the same time you slammed them. In fact the passenger side was a little worse then the driver's side and at times you would have to get out and close it from the outside.

But!! The four-wheel drive worked great that is except for all the strange noises you heard when you backed up in four-wheel drive. So I tried not to do this too often. The boots on the front spindles were in rather bad shape, but half a roll of duct tape and who would ever know.

The bed of the box was a couple of boards, but they were vinyl covered, so they should be good in all weather conditions. The sides of the box (the fenders) were kind of loose, so I built a cover and bolted everything together. This way you were going to lose the whole back half of the truck or nothing. We lost nothing in all the time we drove it.

Power!! Let me tell you this truck had power like no other truck I had ever driven in my life! I mean you could be in either two or four wheel drive, mud, snow, hills or level ground and you never lost a bit of power! In fact one good thing was, you never had to worry about hitting a mud hole with the tires spinning so much you lost all traction and got stuck.

It did not bother me a whole lot, because I had left life in the fast lane of being a game warden, and now had slowed down and was taking it easy. But, it really bothered my boy when we would be heading out hunting, running along about wide open with this baby just humming along, and a party on a riding lawn mower would pull up along side of you, give you a funny, smart-Alec look, and leave you in his dust.

But what could I say; at least I now was the proud owner of my first 4x4 pickup!

Another Year In My Little Red truck

Guess What? My little red truck made it through another hunting season!

Now when you go out in the woods, a person wants to do it right with just a touch of class. So you want to remember that I started out making these trips out in the woods with my Dad in a made over old Ford Model T for a hunting vehicle. Now look what I have!

You would have to take a trip with me someday to really see all the advantages of how a real hunter travels. First you have to get up real early in the morning and one of the first things you do is go out and start the *Red Bomb*. Now it always starts, but only one cylinder at a time. In fact when going from home out to my deer blind, I can almost get to the Three Mile Supper Club before all four cylinders are purring right along.

This past fall I had a new feature develop on my truck. It seems that the valve stems were dry rotting away and this caused the air pressure in the tires to last only about two days before needing a refill. There is no way a true Yooper hunter wants to take the time to fix something like this during the hunting season, so you just stop at the Clark Station every other day for an air refill.

The other thing that happened, for no apparent reason, was when you were humming right along heading out to the woods, the truck would go into convulsions. Jump, jerk, then smooth out and run good for the next couple of days until it happened again. This would make the toughest of Yooper hunters say a prayer, "Dear Lord, please let it run at least through November 30th. (Deer season ends.) The evening of November 30th I pulled into my yard and you would have thought I drove into a sauna! Steam-smoke everywhere, I couldn't see a thing.

I checked it out and found a hose had broke that no normal person could even get at. Somebody had put this hose in the middle of a garage floor over in some foreign country and built a truck around it.

But then I had to stop and remind the Lord that the deer season does not end on November 30th any more with the muzzle-loading season being in the first part of December. So after a good patch job we made it the rest of the way through the hunting season. But so did all the deer.

After the hunting seasons were over, I had to do some hard thinking about my little red truck. I have patched up the exhaust system so many times that the holes now have patches on their patches. But a whole new exhaust system would cost almost $70.00 and this would greatly increase the value of my hunting truck. Maybe three fold. My main concern was wondering if the frame under the truck could hold up all this new piping or would it cause a stress fracture of the frame, therefore ruining my truck.

I sure hated to give up this truck because it has some real advantages. I have yet to hit and kill a bug on its windshield. In all the miles I have traveled with this truck even when it is wound up tight, a bug coming right at you, can still have two choices, either get out of the way before the truck hits it, or land on the front window and just walk over to the side and fly away. What a dream it was, and years later we still laugh about it.

A Question From A Yooper

This falls under something I call the question of the week in some of my weekly articles. It is one of those things I just have trouble figuring out.

Did you ever wonder why, as you drive down the express way or even on the highways up here in the U.P., as those big semi- trucks come flying by you, then cut you off as they pull back in, these trucks that do this never have on the back of their trailer, "How is my driving? Call this 800 number and let me know!"

But those trucks that are driving the speed limit, obey all the road signs, is courteous to others on the road, have this 800 number on the back asking you to call about their driving.

Now, the one you would like to call about does not have the number and the good driver does. Does this make any sense to you? It sure makes a Yooper wonder.

Now the one you would really like to be able to call in about, is the one doing about 90 miles per hour in a 55 zone. Cutting off cars and making a basket case of this Yooper as he tries to put dents in my back license plate following so close. But guess what he is driving?

Here he goes roaring by you in a *"Rent a Truck!"* This scares me all the more, is it like going in and renting a U-haul trailer up here in the U.P. or a wood splitter? Do you have to know how to drive a truck before you can rent a semi-tractor from a *"Rent a Truck?"*

Or do you just fill out a form, pay the guy, and now you are a full-fledged semi-driver? The way some of them drive it sure makes this Yooper wonder!

Before you married that dashing game warden in his uniform!

After putting up with him and his job for twenty years!

Chapter 6
Conservation Officer's Stories
Upper Michigan Tales from a Game Warden's
Perspective
A Yooper's Mentality

It has been a rather interesting project writing my books. Being the student of the English language that I am, this makes for some interesting comments. I was told when I first start out on the book project that I should make sure the stories stayed the same as they were when I first wrote articles for the local paper. People felt that this backwoods, homespun way of telling the stories is what made them so popular with people from all over the country. But, the one thing you must understand is the fact that the way I write stories is the way I am. I could not be any other way if I wanted to.

My sister from Wisconsin was up at our house visiting with her husband and an exchange student from Hungary. On Saturday evening this girl went with us to the youth's activity at church. I had her tell the other teenagers a little about herself so she told them where she was from and that she could speak four different languages. But, she said, "Of all of them I speak, English was the hardest to learn." I could have told her that! In fact I did tell her what makes it worse is the fact that we "Yooper's" living here in the U. P. have our own dialect of the English language that foreigners just don't understand.

The following may help you better understand something about us Yooper's.

Understanding The Yooper Dialect

It's both interesting and hard to put my books together. First I type out a rough copy of the story I am working on. Then I go over it a dozen times till it gets where I want it. Then I have someone go over it for me and I correct it. After this correction is done another lady goes over it for me. I correct it again and then a gal down at A&J Printing puts it in book form on a computer. It is printed out in page form and sent back to me for a final going over.

Finally the day arrives when the proofs for the book, all laid out in book form, are sent back to me for the 'ok' before they go ahead and print the books. The first thing you want to do when these proofs of my tales arrive is to make sure all the English teachers in the U.P. are out in the middle of Lake Michigan on a slow boat trip. I can't figure out for the life of me why this always seems to work out best, but if you have read any of my stories maybe you could make a good guess.

When this happens there are usually four of us going over it this time, but I will not say who to protect their reputation with the English language. It is really hard to do when you don't want to change the homespun way the stories are written. One of them always tells me, " The rule says, English rule that is, you don't do this after this unless it's before this!" I always tell them, "Now, that may be true according to the person that wrote the rule book you go by, but now how do we know that rule book is right?" "It just may be that the person who wrote this rule book, just used another rule book to go by. So how do we know if the first one was right either?" "And, if the truths were known probably neither one of these writers ever lived in the U.P. to start with." "And, if they did, I'm sure they were just too busy writing this rule book to confuse all us normal Yooper's, they never had time to go to hunting camp and tell stories like all normal Yoopers do!"

About this time I sure get the same feeling old Dizzy Dean must have felt back in that old black and white movie.

But there is hope!

I finally had to break down and buy a computer with all the modern gadgets on it for my book business. In fact it even has one of these things called grammar check. (I assume this is when grandma sits down and helps you with your schoolwork.) So to make sure I was doing everything right, I took one of my stories and put it through grandma's check and you know what? I was right all the time!

This new gadget said about the wording of my tales, "Normally this word is not used in this context or this format." Now, the key word to this whole thing is the word <u>normally!</u> If you read this like you are supposed to, it does not tell you, you cannot use this word like you did. It just says according to the rules it could be wrong to do. So, if you are a normal person, leading a normal life, but then there are the rest of us... So there is hope for normal Yoopers with a Yooper's dialect yet!

Just so you will understand here are a few items to help you out.

A Yooper's Wisdom

Ifen, you know that the "Big Mac" is something you drive across not eat, you must be a true Yooper.

Ifen, you think every room in your house should have something with a touch of hunter's orange in it; you must be a true Yooper.

Ifen, you think that the colors green and gold go with the fall and winter seasons in the U.P. you must be a true Yooper.

Ifen, you believe that "down south" refers to Lower Michigan or Wisconsin; you must be a true Yooper.

Ifen, you use a rag for a gas cap, you must own a true Yooper- type vehicle.

Ifen, you have seen a little league game snowed out, you must be a true Yooper.

Ifen, you know what a pasty is and Mom bakes them, you must be a true Yooper.

Ifen, you know that Mackinac and Mackinaw are one and the same; you must be a true Yooper.

Ifen, you keep a window scraper in your car all year around, you must be a true Yooper.

Ifen, you think Alkaline batteries were named after a Detroit Tiger outfielder; you must be a true Yooper.

Ifen, you know what Vernor's is and you use it when the kids are sick, you must be a true Yooper.

Ifen, you know that traveling from coast to coast is to travel from Lake Superior to Lake Michigan; you must be a true Yooper.

Ifen, half the change in your pocket is Canadian, you must be a true Yooper.

Ifen, you know there are only two seasons in Michigan, winter and Construction; you must be a true Yooper.

Ifen, your worst nightmare is learning to time traffic lights, you must be a true Yooper.

Ifen, none of the lights on your snowmobile or boat trailer work, but you plan on fixing them first chance you remember, you must be a true Yooper.

Ifen, wifee's *"honey do"* projects outnumber the days there are from the last snowfall in the spring till the first snowfall in the fall, you are a true Yooper with a normal problem.

Ifen, you think that the big G on your favorite football team's uniform stands for God's Team; you must be a true Yooper.

Ifen, you had any kids born between November 15th and the 30th you are a true Yooper that flunked math. Or you are still blaming it on bad water.

Ifen, the main color on your pickup is Bondo, you must be a true Yooper.

Ifen, you still collect 8-track tapes at yard sales, you must be a true Yooper.

Ifen, you were ever fired from a construction job for sloppy dress; you must be a true Yooper.

Ifen, your dog and wallet are both on a chain; you must be a true Yooper.

Ifen, there are more 4x4 pickups at a funeral than cars; you must be a true Yooper.

Ifen, your Mom walks you to school then spends all day with you cause you are in the same grade, you must be a true Yooper.

Ifen, you wear a cowboy hat to church, you must be a true Yooper that is lost.

Ifen, you believe that true recycling is using worn out tires on your pickup, from a buddy's vehicle, you must be a true Yooper.

Ifen, you have an old, moth eaten deer head hanging in your living room, you must be a true Yooper.

Ifen, like Eino after listening to the weather on the U. P. weather reports, you know less then before you head it, you must be a True Yooper. "There is a fifty-fifty chance for snow today." Eino wonders does this mean there is or there isn't, do I wear my long handles and boots or don't I?

Ifen, in the summer for Eino things get better right? "Today it will start out being partly cloudy in the morning, till late afternoon when it will then be partly sunny." Do I wear my shades, or leave them at home? He is still a confused True Yooper.

A Yooper Mother Writing Her Son At College

Dear Son;

I am writing this letter real slow 'cause I know you can't read too fast. We don't live where we did when you went off to college. Your dad read in the paper that most pickup accidents happened within twenty miles of home, so we moved. I can't send you our new address as the last Yooper family that lived here took the house numbers with them, they plan to use them on their new house so they won't have to change their address and confuse everything.

This place has one of those auto-matic washing machines I read about. But the first day here I used it, I put in four shirts and pulled the chain, and haven't seen them since, but when they do return they ought to really be clean.

It only snowed here twice last week, three days the first time and four days the second time. About the heavy winter coat you wanted me to send you, Aunt Sue said it would be a little too heavy to send by mail with those heavy brass buttons on it, so we cut them off and placed them in the left hand jacket pocket for you, along with a needle and some thread so you can sew them back on. By the way, we got a bill from the funeral home last week, it said if we didn't make the last payment on Grandma's funeral, up she comes!

About your older sister, she had her baby this morning. I haven't made it up to the hospital yet to find out if it's a boy or a girl, so I don't know if you're an aunt or an uncle yet. Your uncle John fell off the walkway at work into one of the whiskey vats and drowned. Some of the men at work tried to pull him out, but he fought them off. We had his body cremated and he burned with a bright blue flame for three days till the fire department came by and put it out.

Three of your cousins went off the old bridge over the river in their pickup truck, one was driving and the other two were riding in the back in the truck box. The driver got out all right; he rolled down the window and swam to safety. Your other two cousins were not as lucky; they could not get the tailgate open in time to get out.

Aunt Hazel's knitting you some socks, she would have mailed them out last week, but I reminded her that you wrote and told me you had grown a foot since you left home for college. So she is knitting you another one so all three will match.

Not much more going on up here. O' by the way, your brother locked his keys in the car at the house the other day. It sure was a mess 'cause it took him three days to get a door open and get his family out! On top of that we had rain and snow mixed during that time and he couldn't get into the car to put the top up! But everything's all right now.

Well, right soon, MOM

Chapter 7

Conservation Officer's Stories
Upper Michigan Tales from a Game Warden's Perspective

An Outdoor Man's Love Story

Kid's Please Listen!

I guess one of the greatest things about being a Game Warden was all the nice people you came across in your travels. The interesting thing is, when I went out on my book project this just continued on. I have stated a number of times, "The best thing about writing my books is all the friends I have made through them."

This is the case with the gentleman in this chapter. I had never met outdoor writer Ed Erickson while still working as a Conservation Officer even though I had heard of him. He has for years been one of the most respected outdoor writers in the U.P.

One day while traveling with my books and hoping to get newspapers to write a little article telling people about them, I stopped at the newspaper in Iron River called the Reporter. I asked the lady at the front desk if I could talk to someone about my books to see if they would be willing to do an article on them. She led me into a little back office where I met Ed Erickson for the first time.

I was introduced to a great big guy with a firm handshake, and a grin from one side of his face to the other. After talking to Ed for a few minutes I soon found out that he was my kind of guy. We talked that first day for a couple of hours it seemed and then he did a real nice article about my books.

Later I was to speak at a Father-Son Banquet at the First Baptist Church in Iron River and once again Ed did a great article titled, *"Retired game warden, Telling Tales about Life, Lads, and the Lord"* This past fall I stopped in to see him once again because I wanted him to read over my pamphlet about using the outdoors to help parents to raise their kids.

Once again we talked for quite a while and I left him a copy of my pamphlet, *A Quiver Full.* I knew how this man for years had fought the battle of trying to save the outdoors for other sportsmen to use as we have enjoyed it for years. I think after talking to him for hours like I had, I knew his heart, his love for family, God, and the U.P. So I wanted him to give me some honest advice.

After reading things over he wrote me a nice letter and one of the things he said was he could see my love for my Dad in what I write. He also told me about his youngest son, Kyle, and how they had this same type bond of fellowship together. When I read this letter from him I never dreamt I would receive the following letter a few short months later. After you read his letter I want to tell you a few things about and from a father's heart.

Feb. 11, 1998

Dear John,

It has been some time since we visited. I always appreciated the stories you told about your Dad when you were young. I could sense you had a deep love for your Dad and he for you. It was heart-warming then and meaningful to me now as you related to your Dad.

I don't know if you are aware of it or not, but the situation is reversed with me and my youngest son. I am still here, but Kyle went to be with the Lord on Dec. 10, 1997. He was survey crew chief for Sundberg, Carlson, and Associates in its Iron River office. He and his survey partner were taking some final measurements for the new Iron County Community Hospital between Iron River and Crystal Falls. With a tape in hand, he was killed instantly when a pickup truck hit him. Every time Eunice and I go by the site, we call it Kyles's launching pad.

Kyle was 29. Being the youngest of five boys, he and I were incredibly close. I got him fishing at a young age. We hunted together all his short life. He killed a nine-point buck at age 14. After he gained confidence and stature, his personality bloomed. He was the sparkplug and enthusiastic promoter at deer camp. Kyle kept us all fired up. The last few years, he was my mentor, my hero.

Even though he went off to college, graduating from NMU in 1991 with a BS degree in zoology and wildlife biology, we continued to stay close after that. Kyle got married and had a daughter. They bought our former home on US-2 just west of IR. I saw him at least once a week and we talked on the telephone at least two, three times a week. We about shared everything. Like you and your dad, we enjoyed many hours together. I used to tell him a lot of the stories you told me and some from your books.

What we are grateful for was Kyle enjoyed zest for life, especially the outdoors. Moreover, he loved the Lord and his family. Even though he has been gone for only two months, it is so empty and lonely without him. All our hunting and fishing plans for 1998 and beyond are shattered.

But then we accept the reality that Kyle's homecoming was part of God's perfect plan for his life on earth and eternity.

I'm enclosing a couple of articles about Kyle I thought you might enjoy reading, given the closeness you had with your Dad.

Your friend in Christ,

A Dad To His Son,
To Son Kyle

If we never...
> *Flush another woodcock,*
> *Train another dog,*
> *Catch another walleye,*
> *Spear another northern,*
> *Hook another brookie,*
> *Bag another grouse,*
> *Set another trap,*
> *Scout another deer trail,*
> *Smell another scrape,*
> *Admire another rub,*
> *Sight another rifle,*
> *Skin another buck,*
> *Our partnership with each other,*
> *And with the out of doors,*
> *Will have been complete,*
> *Because most of all,*
> *You are my Pard.*
> > *Love, Dad (1991)*

From the old Drummer, Ed Erickson III, his newspaper articles are called *The Drumming Log.*

On December 10, 1997, God chose to take my son, my pard, to be with Him. The parting has not been easy. At every turn around the log, there are mementos of his vigor and enthusiasm for life and his incredible appreciation for the out of doors.

Over the 29 years the Lord loaned Kyle to us, I discovered early in his young life the zeal he had for just being outdoors. We'd walk and talk. He was full of questions. When he was a little squirt, he'd ride on my shoulders with his head amongst the branches of the trees. "I can get a better look from up here, Dad," he'd say.

When he was a boy we fished a little bit. The family nest was so full of children, there wasn't much time to get really involved with other outdoor recreational sports. I'd tell him hunting and trapping stories of when I was a lad. When Kyle was age 11, he asked, "Why don't we go hunting, Dad?"

That spark of encouragement was enough to get me back into the brush. When Kyle was 11, I shot a buck with him at my side. Three years later, age 14, Kyle killed his first buck-a nine pointer off the 900 Road in southwest Iron County.

Over the years, we were partners in trout fishing, ruffed grouse and woodcock hunting, more deer hunting; trapping weasels, muskrat and beaver; fishing for walleye and spearing northern through the ice; building tree stands; camping out since 1981, staying at camp.

Without reservation, I can truthfully say that over the 29 years of joy and satisfaction of being partners in the woods, in the stream, on the lake, and at camp, we never had an argument. We never had a disagreement of any kind, ever!

Klye, was the last one to write in the deer camp log on Nov. 30. To us left behind, he wrote a game plan for the 1998 hunting season on how to get the big bucks northwest of Lake 22, our hunting turf he appreciated so much.

Today, I can almost hear Kyle say, "I can get a better look from up here, Dad."

Son To Dad

After Kyle's death this was found on his computer as the dedication for a book he was working on called, *The Hunter.*

"This book is dedicated to my Mom. She's the one that sheds tears of joy; the one that brings emotion into the sport of hunting; the one that shows and restores the memories of these hunts just by taking pictures."

"This book is dedicated to my wife and daughter; the ones that patiently wait for me to come home after a hunt; the ones that leave my supper warm; the ones that don't get the time I spend to hunt. It's a shame."

"This book is also dedicated to my Dad; the one that made it all possible for me to hunt; the one that spent endless hours, days, and years teaching me the ways of the whitetail deer. He is the one that taught me respect for the animals; the one that disciplined me on ethics; the one that shared his time with me instead of spending it with others; the one that field dressed my first deer; the one that gave me endless literature to educate me more and more; the one that photographed all the deer I have taken; the one that brought the love of the sport into my life."

"I love deer to hunt deer, but most of all I love my Dad. Thanks Dad for Sharing"

(This basically is all Kyle got done on his book prior to his tragic death.)

....

I hope and pray that those that read this chapter can see the bond that was able to be built between a father and son by the time they spent in the great out of doors together. This is why I have called this, *A Love Story From an Outdoor Man's Heart.*

So parents, please take the time to give your kids a hug and tell them you love them. Also kids, please give Mom and Dad a hug, tell them you love them, because we just never know how long it will be before all we have to live with is the memories we have built together. Make them good ones.

Kyle Erickson, then age 21, killed this eight-point buck in western Iron County in 1989. Kyle shared the drama of harvesting this buck, along with many years of other experiences in the outdoors, with his dad Ed Erickson III (right) of Iron River. Kyle went to be with the Lord on Dec. 10, 1997, immediately after being killed in a vehicle/pedestrian accident.

A Quiver Full
(Hey Son Lets Have a little Talk)

A Game Warden's Perspective on Child Rearing
By Sgt. John A. Walker

Chapter 8
Conservation Officer's Stories
Upper Michigan Tales from a Game Warden's Perspective
A Quiver Full

(This is an outline for a seminar given on using the outdoors to teach family values. Sgt. John A. Walker is a retired Michigan Conservation Officer and the author of a number of books of family-style humorous outdoor tales.) Pamphlets containing this chapter can be ordered from J.A.W.'S Publications.

....

I guess there is not a parent in the world that does not have at least a zillion dreams for their children as they watch them grow up in this old world. It seems that if our children can just meet some of our dreams we can count our project of being a parent as having been successful.

One of the most interesting and true facts, which I have learned during all my travels through life, is the fact that every young person, when growing up needs a *buddy*. If a young person does not find the right kind of a friend to be their buddy that will help them walk down the straight path of life into being a successful adult, you can surely bet they will find a buddy that will lead and help them to follow that other path that will lead them down, down, down.

First off please let me tell you a few things about myself. I have observed and learned the things I am writing about after working as an outdoor recreation safety instructor for more than thirty years. Also, for over the past twenty years I have worked as the youth director at the church my family and I attend. During this time there have been hundreds and hundreds of youth cross my path.

For more than twenty years my wife and I have made a trip each summer with teenagers down to the Bill Rice Ranch located at Murfreesboro, Tenn. We have taken youth from all over a three-state area on this trip with us. After getting to the ranch a week is spent with youth from all over the country. You soon learn after spending all this time with teenagers that they have some special needs that only a buddy can fill.

We can now get started into how to use hunting, fishing, and the great outdoors to our advantage. This while trying to help youth to grow up straight and true. Please let me point out a few things.

In the Bible, Psalm 127:4-5 reads: *"As arrows are in the hand of a mighty man; so are children of our youth. Happy is the man that has a quiver full of them."*

Now as we all know some families have single shot quivers. Some hold two or three arrows, and some can even hold a dozen arrows or more. They, the arrows in the quiver that is, seem to come in all sizes. But, they are all something special and they all need someone that will take the time to love them and help them through the steps of growing up. This is where we can come in.

I heard a man say something at an outdoor show one time that stuck in my mind and really got me thinking. I have talked this very subject over with dozens and dozens of parents. He stated, *"All of us carry arrows around in our quivers, we look them over, we check them for flaws, we practice with them to make sure that their flit is straight and true, in other words we spend time with our bow and arrows to try and perfect the end results. But, if we have a quiver full of arrows where these arrows never leave the quiver to fulfill their purpose, or that are never made use of, what good are they to anyone? An arrow is made for a purpose and so is each youth we come across in our lives."*

In other words a dad and mom must take the time to practice with and train up the youth that are in their quiver. For that day will come, as it already has for so many of us, when every dad will have to nock that arrow out of their quiver, draw back on that bow with all their strengths, and release that arrow of theirs to fly off at whatever goal or target lays down the road before them. As a parent we can only hope and pray that the time spent in checking over our arrows, in all the practice with them, all the training that has went into their life, will cause the arrow to fly straight and true to the target. This will lead to a happy and successful life for them down the road when they are out on their own. It is every parent's dream, but it does not always come easy.

Please let me point out a few things for you that just may help you out.

Some time back, I was talking to a real successful businessman. As we were talking, I made this statement to him. *"You know so many people do not really understand hunters and fishermen. It is not always the idea we have to get or take something, but just the idea we are lucky enough to just get to be out in the backwoods . . ."* I went on to say, *"Isn't it funny, but you can read a book sitting at home and that is one thing, or you can read the same book sitting out in the woods against a tree with a fishing pole, or sitting in your hunting camp over a cup of coffee during a deer season and it is a whole different world."*

Did you ever notice how great toast made over an open flame on a gas-stove taste? It is so much better, even if the toast is burnt black out at camp. This camp toast is still better than that perfectly browned toast made in the gadget on the counter back home!

It has to be the attitude toward what is taking place and the atmosphere around it. For there is nothing else that can explain it. So, don't you think it is important to stop for a minute and realize that if you feel this way under these conditions, just maybe it would be a good place to use as a tool in rising your youth? *(If you read the books I have authored you will soon see where I get a lot of my ideas. My Dad used these tools with all his kids as we were growing up and it worked.)*

A-Always remember if it's special to you, make it special to them too

As you travel through life with your kids, make sure they learn how you truly feel about the great outdoors. Have some special areas where the two of you can spend time, just getting close to each other. It could be a fishing hole, a beaver dam where the ducks come in, a ridge you walk along looking for deer signs. It does not really matter where it is; just that it is a special place for friendship. I can still picture places in my mind that my dad and I checked out year after year, almost fifty years ago.

Talk to them, take the time to explain the reason you have learned to like this certain place. Tell them about your memories that are there. Build a place in *their* heart so that whenever you are together with them spending time, being a buddy, they will feel free to talk to you about whatever is on their mind.

(My oldest boy when he was home from college with his girlfriend took her for a ride up to the old hunting camp. This is where his grandfather is buried. It was one of these special places I am talking about. While showing this pretty, young girl from Iowa where Grandpa was buried, he asked her to marry him. Corny, yes, but still it added to a young man's feelings at this important time in his life.)

It could also be a certain hunting item that has been handed down through the years that you got from your dad and later passed on to your son. I can recall this taking place as plain today as when it happened more than forty years ago.

One night my Dad was sitting in his chair. This was way before the age of recliners and my Dad had a footstool that had a lid on it. Inside his footstool he stored all his old pictures and personal items he wanted to keep. There were a few old tintype pictures, some odds and ends from his family, and an old, knit, red hunting cap that had been his Dad's.

On this night, my dad was looking through his collection and came across this cap that had been his Dad's. As I watched, as a teenage boy, my dad picked up the old, red, knit, hunting cap and leaned back in his chair. Then it was as if his mind left the room we were in, to travel back to all those good old times when he and his Dad spent time out in the woods together. As this young man sat there with his Dad now, he saw a couple of tears run down his dad's cheeks as his Dad held his Dad's old hunting cap. I did not have to ask him what was the matter for I knew what he was thinking. Now this same old red hunting cap is still around and has passed from me down to one of my boys. There were a whole lot of good memories traveling along with this old, red, hunting cap.

Let your children and outdoor buddies know how you feel about getting out in the woods and why it is special to you. Let them see you are a *real* person with feelings that they can understand. Build these same feelings in them.

B-Be their buddy

Always remember that while they are out in the great outdoors with you, they are not only your children, but are also your buddies. There is a difference you know. A lot of people have kids, but very few people go through life with the rapport that being someone's buddy builds. When you do this, you are on your way to having a successful project as a parent. Your goal should be in building this feeling up, so if and when they ever get where they need some advice, in their walk through life, they will come to their *buddy* (you) for it. I don't think there is any better feeling for a parent, than when one of their children (or an outdoor buddy) feels that they can come to the one that they know loves them for help and guidance. If they don't come to you for it, it can be downright scary when you stop and think who and where they may go off to for help.

Building this feeling is a project that never ends. It can start from the time you have something special in your pocket for them when you come home from work, till the time they leave the nest and go out on their own. Letting someone know you really care about them and want to help them as they travel through life is hard. This is why it is so important to be their *buddy*.

C-Let them know that Wifee (Mother) is someone special:

Let your children know just how their parents feel about each other. As you are walking through the woods or just sitting out at camp with them, make it a point to let them know how you feel about your spouse. Let them hear you say what you value about each other and how they should appreciate all the *"other half"* does for the family.

I think this is one of the most amazing things I ever heard. I was sitting at a wedding reception with some friends and their teenage children. As we were talking about the families and life in the home with the kids, one of their older, teenage daughters made the statement that she had never in all her life ever heard her parents say they loved each other!! What a shame for a teenager to be able to say this! The parents who were sitting right there both agreed with what their daughter had just said. I thought to myself, what a shame for any family to be able to say something like this.

What a time to teach your children to respect and appreciate the feeling and rights of each other. I have observed ladies, who were beautiful enough to be models, get a tremendous kick out of the fact their husband got his first bear or deer. Doing this even if they themselves would never go hunting in a million years. But by the same token, I have observed a husband on a hunting trip pick up a little something special for Wifee back home. Our hunter just wanted to let her know he cared and was thinking about her. Let your kids see your heart when you do these things.

D-Dads. Remember that no two children are alike:

Dads, remember to have patience with all your kids. Remember not just the one that has the natural ability to do everything, but all of them. I have observed it so many times, where one child can do almost every outdoor activity without having to really try. This while another child (as my Dad always said) "could not hit the barn if they were standing inside it shooting their gun!" Some kids will just take that little extra time to be able to hit what they are shooting at or to catch a fish without hooking half dozen trees first. But remember they too need your love, patience, and attention. Please don't make everything a contest between your kids. In fact it would be better to have the contest between dad and the kids, rather then between the kids themselves. For dad, that day will arrive like it has already for so many of us, when dad no longer always wins that contest between dad and the kids. In fact as the years roll by dad may have to redo the rules now and then to give him a better chance of winning once in a while.

But, remember no two kids are alike! One may just have the natural talent to pull up with a shotgun and break that clay pigeon the first time they try. While the other one may be more interested in the how and why of what takes place. But they all have a place in our hearts and they should go to bed every night knowing it.

Please always remember, you can go out and buy a dozen arrows and for some reason no two seem to shoot exactly alike. For some reason it always seems there are one or two that just shoot a little straighter and truer than the rest do. If no two arrows in your hunting quiver are exactly the same, when they are machine made, why should our kids be, when they come from usens who are not exactly alike.

E-Remember, you are now a teacher, be patient:

I am sitting here and I have to laugh to myself as I write about this. I can remember back more than forty years ago sitting in a boat fishing with my grandpa one evening. We were up in the canal off Hancock, and I was at the age when everything he did I had to ask him, "Why?" Then after he answered that question there would be at least a dozen more questions come up in my youthful mind. After a while grandpa looked at me and said, "Johnny, why don't you take a minute before you ask all those questions and think them over before you ask them?" You know those words of advice cut those dumb questions at least in half! But, I can never remember grandpa or my dad getting mad at all the crazy questions I must have asked them. It was a good lesson learned.

As you are walking through the woods with them, if you see something that is pretty or interesting to you, stop and take a minute to point it out to them. Also, take the time to explain it to them. Be sure to be ready to answer all their questions as you open up their young minds. Please, don't let them be scared to ask questions of you.

I have to laugh at all the questions that come up in young minds after the lights are turned off out at camp. It seems as the lights go off, their minds open up recalling the day's activities. What better place and time to let them think that dad is just about the smartest guy in the whole wide world? Don't worry as the years go by they will soon outgrow the feeling.

I used to always tell my kids, when they asked me one of their famous questions and wanted to know how I knew all I did, "Because Conservation Officers just know about everything there is for a person to know!" Now, after they have been through college and have families of their own, they will call to ask me a question that a rocket scientist could never answer. When I tell them this they always say, "Come on Dad, you always told us that Conservation Officers know everything!" But I guess they don't understand that after you retire you no longer have that ability.

Always take time to answer their questions and explain things to them.

F-Remember your feelings are showing:

I guess this ties into all the rest of the areas I have covered. But I want to put a little more weight on this with a few more thoughts. For some reason it seems that an outdoor person has to be such a macho person. They feel they cannot convey their feelings to their kids or else it is a sign of weakness. This scares me.

Let your little hunting buddies see your heart and what really makes you tick as far as the great outdoors goes. Explain to them why you do things the way you do them. Why you never leave litter in the area you travel through. Why you even take time to pick up someone else's litter and how it bugs you when people come to a pretty spot in the woods and leave a mess.

Teach them to get a hunting and fishing guide each year and to go over it. Talk to them about the way things used to be and why there are so many changes in the outdoors now. Always remember that they are the watchers, don't throw everything you have built up all the rest of the year away teaching them right from wrong, over a silly deer or fish.

I have observed it dozens of times where a dad would never steal or cheat around town or at work. But, let him get out in the woods and there is a whole different set of rules. I have watched this same dad trying to figure out why his kids later in life were always in trouble and laws meant nothing to them. It appears they did not draw the line the same place dad did. For dad it was an undersize fish, a pat out of season or one too many, an illegal deer. But for the kids it was stealing some baseball cards, wrecking some flower boxes up town, etc.

The old saying, *"Don't do as I do, do as I say"* never worked and it never will, especially out in the great outdoors with nobody watching.

G-Build memories:

In closing, please let me say that all through life we are building memories for our kids. What kind are you leaving yours with?

If you have read the four books, I have written you have read what kind my parents left me. Great ones.

If your buddies do something wrong out in the woods while with you, correct them about it. But, at the same time explain to them why you are correcting them. Use this as a tool to teach them something. Build something they will pass on to those they will hunt with years later. If you handle it right, I can just hear the tales that will come out of this experience ten years down the road. In fact I have been known to write a book or two about some of these tales.

How many times have you sat around a hunting camp with the old crew and spent hours going over the memories of growing up and the crazy things that happened? As I wrote in one of my books, "When dad says, *you know the other day...* and starts in on one of his tales, it is really hard to tell what decade the tale he is telling came from." The old hunting and fishing memories never get old. They just get better with the passing of the years. I told my boy Rob one day at camp, *"Son, someday all that you will have from me are the memories of our time spent together. It will matter little if you or I got a deer every year. What will matter as you grow older and sit where I am sitting now with your kids someday, is what tales can you tell them that will start, "You know the other day grandpa and I were......."*

So there you have it, a few thoughts that may help you make it easier for those from your quiver shoot a little straighter and truer as they go through life. As I have said before, *"Being a parent is a project and something that must be worked at."* I hope what is talked about in this article may help you out just a little in using the tools the Good Lord gave us here on earth.

So Dad, nock those arrows of yours when the times comes, (family or just a buddy you're trying to help out, hopefully both) pull back as hard as one can, aim at a goal or target for your arrow and let fly!

If you as their *buddy* have checked over the arrow for any flaws, did your best to correct them. If you spent time together practicing before this day came. You did all that anyone can do, as a *buddy*. So let fly, it is now out of your hands. It is now in *His* hands to take over and direct your arrows the rest of the way through life.

When this happens, your heart will feel like it is coming up into your throat, you will walk through their bedroom with a tear in your eye and an ache in your chest, knowing things will never be the same again. But, if you can truly have the satisfaction and feeling, "I gave them my best shot, now it is up to them." You will then be a winner.

Each one of the books written by Sgt. Walker has a chapter in it teaching something about the home and family values.

A Deer Gets Revenge
(The Old Fashioned way)

This chapter in Sgt. Walker's first book talks about how to raise kids the old fashioned way. It tells about doing things with them and making them feel important to Mom and Dad. It covers some of the family things that Sgt. Walker went through while growing up. It ends with the Walker Kid's doing what their Dad always wanted, both Mom and Dad are buried up in a little cemetery under big oak tree at hunting camp in his home town.

(Christmas in the U.P.)

In this chapter Sgt. Walker tells about how Christmas used to be in the backwoods during the end of the forties and early fifties. He talks about making things for each other (seeing you could not afford to buy gifts) and the fact that a family can have a great Christmas even if they do not have a whole lot of material things. If a Christmas is wrapped in the love that a Mom and Dad feel for their children nothing else really matters.

A Bucket of Bones
(My Dad, My Hero)

This book starts out with the poem "Builder of Bridges" by W.A. Dromgool.

In this chapter of his second book Sgt. Walker covers a number of things that his Dad taught him while they were out in the woods doing things together and just being buddies. He points out the fact that it is a whole lot easier to communicate with youth when you are not only a parent, but also their buddy. He tells about the fact that the great outdoors is a wonderful place to use to teach your kids things that will help them out all through life once they are out on their own away from the nest.

Sgt. Walker covers a number of times later in life when these lessons taught by Dad help him to make the right decision.

(Kid's You're Special)

In this chapter *(Guardian Angels Do Go Hunting)* Sgt. Walker talks to teenagers. When Sgt. Walker found out that so many moms and youth were reading his books, he felt they could be used to talk to young people about things they should hear. In this section he tells a true tale about how one of his boys almost drowned while out duck hunting with a buddy. The spin off of this is to tell youth they are special to both Mom and Dad, and they do love them, and would surely miss them if something ever happened to them.

The chapter ends with an article from a newspaper he has had for over twenty-five years warning teenagers. The article titled *I'm Only 17* speaks to the hearts of teenagers.

From the Land Where BIG Fish Live

This book starts out with a writing by Douglas MacArthur titled, <u>A Father's Prayer.</u>

(My Mom, Dad, and Tim)

In this, his third book, Sgt. Walker tells about his brother Tim who had brain damage as a baby. He talks about Mom, Dad, and the fact that the rest of the family that never heard a word of complaint about the special job having a son like Tim was. This tale tells about the heart of Sgt. Walker's Mom, Dad, and Tim's family.

Sgt. Walker also has a number of tales in this book about things that happened in his family while growing up in the backwoods. Women and kids seem to really love these tales and the way they are written.

Luck, Skill, or Just Maybe Stupidity
(A Game Warden's Wifee)

After receiving so many requests for him to write some tales about what it must be like to be married to a Game Warden, Sgt. Walker includes a number of tales about being his wifee in this, his forth book. Sometimes it is unreal what a wifee has to go through when married for better or for worse.

(Vietnam Spreads A Shadow Over Ontonagon)

In this book Sgt. Walker includes an article written by an AP reporter about Ontonagon, his hometown, during the Vietnam War. He feels this article shows the heart, soul, and character of youth from the U.P. This article was written about a couple of his high school buddies who were killed over in Vietnam. One was killed while trying to save his sergeant, and his high school buddy was killed while trying to save him. Two small town high school buddies killed on the other side of the world together. Sgt. Walker has been told by a number of people that they could not read this chapter without shedding a tear or two.

Kids Please Listen
(The Empty Rocking Chair)

This book ends with Sgt. Walker once again speaking to youth about family values. He talks about his buddy, his Dad, and their time spent together and how special it was. In closing, he tells about the empty rocking chair now out at hunting camp that used to be Dad's. Also about the fact that life does go on, but it goes on with something missing from his heart. So enjoy your Dad while he is around and you are able to.

Humans are Nuts!
(And we call it fun!)

This fifth book has a chapter that tells the real love a father and son can build thru the time they spend hunting and fishing together.

A Love Story From an Outdoor's Man's Heart

All that this story covers about Kyle and his dad are from items the two of them had written. In some cases, items the other had not know about until after Kyle's untimely death while at work.

Only the letters Sgt. Walker receives tell the true way the books Sgt. Walkers writes are accepted and enjoyed. People from all over the country write him, a person they have never met, to tell Sgt. Walker about how they feel they know him and his family. These letters have went even so far as to include prayer requests from families who have read his books.

One reason for this could be the down-to-earth, family-style way these tales are told. As Sgt. Walker tells people, "Its just like Grandpa used to tell his grandkids stories years ago, before TV came along and ruined all these great story telling times."

Chapter 9
Conservation Officer's Stories
Upper Michigan Tales from a Game Warden's Perspective
My Opinion 1-4

In each of my last three books I have had a chapter titled *My Opinion.* That is exactly what this chapter is, some of the things I learn in my travels and working as a game warden. It is no secret that I feel there are just to many *Exspurts* running around this world. Where is the good old common sense and that good old wisdom that causes all that gray hair.

Where have all the perch gone?

The one thing I do hear in my travels, around the U.P. and Northern Wisconsin with my bookmobile, is what happened to all the good perch fishing in some areas? It seems like in the last few years the perch fishing, especially in Lake Michigan, has been going downhill. I have read a number of articles about this and even received a number of letters on it.

The one thing you can say about my book project is that you sure get to meet and talk to a lot of people. This plus the fact that a lot of people just want someone to tell their theory too. I must say that when hearing from all these people I have to stop a minute and think about two things. Number one: when people from all over the area I travel, from all walks of life, have the same reasons they give for what is taking place, just maybe we should stop to think about it for a minute. Number two: when people have spent their whole life working and living in an area, sometimes, their wisdom accumulated throughout the years should just maybe be added into the equation. From these facts come the two following theories I place under the category *"Food for thought"*.

Number One: This is nothing new whether it be on the land or in the water and I have stated it before, *"When we totally protect one specie of birds or animals it is always at the detriment of another specie."* This is no different when it comes to fish. I have heard over and over from Green Bay to Drummond Island that, "We had better do something about all the Comarants!" It is the feeling of a whole lot of people that these birds have gotten way out of control in a lot of areas. In fact, I hear the same thing from Florida to Michigan in my travels.

I have had people tell me that they can sit on their deck in the early morning in the last few years and can watch hundreds and hundreds of Comarants fishing in wave after wave each and every morning. They say where there used to be a few now there are just way too many. I have been told that they will come across a bay in waves in the early morning, one wave diving in for the fish, as another waves goes over the top of the first wave of birds already in the water, to hit the water in front of them for fish. People tell me this goes back and forth all morning, day in and day out.

One statement made to me was this, "You can blame the Indians all you want for the poor fishing, but these birds take tons more fish then the Indians ever could."

I personally have to give some credence to this after seeing how many Comarants there are living on the islands in some areas. We have, through our methods of overly protecting things, thrown nature way out of balance in some areas.

The other thing that has happened, and some of this I have observed myself in my travels, is this. Years ago, whether we agreed with the use of gill nets or not, these fishermen took tons and tons of trash fish out of the waters where the perch lived. I have been at the docks as commercial tugs pulled in years ago after lifting their nets to be loaded with tons of suckers. Needless to say they were not happy campers after lifting all these suckers and only getting a few cents a pound for them, but they did remove a lot of them from the lakes. There were also a lot of carp, lawyers, (the fish) and other trash fish taken by these commercial fishermen. But, today we have stopped the commercial fishermen from using gill nets in most areas and to a lot of people the trash fish are way over what is a good balance.

Let me explain what has been told to me and then you can run it through that computer between your ears.

It goes this way; there is just so much area out in the lakes to support each fish that lives there. There is just so much food in the food chain, so much spawning area, and all the other things needed to keep a good supply of sport fish. If these areas are way over populated with trash fish someone else has to pay for it. If carp, suckers, lawyers, dogfish, etc. are taking up this limited space out in the eco chain in the lake, just where are the perch going to live?

The problem as a lot of people see it, is the fact that most of these trash fish have nothing that keeps their population in check. In small inland lakes we can poison them off and re-plant to balance things off again. But what do we do in the Great lakes?

I could explain some more on these two items, but I figure there is enough here to be *"Food for thought."*

My Opinion-2
The new way that things are done

Now that small game season is open there seems to be a few more people running around the woods. I have to wonder if a body stops to think about how many laws or interpretation of laws a person could be breaking just by leaving his yard? This past weekend I was at an outdoor show next to a party that sold go-cart type vehicles for running around the woods with. I had to ask myself, "Just where in the world could a person even operate one of these without wondering how long before he was in deep trouble with someone."

Let me explain what scares me in this day and age. We all used to laugh, and still do, about the fact that six people could call the same IRS office and ask the same question as a taxpayer and come up with six different answers on the same law from the same organization. I think this disease has now spread to other government agencies. And when this happens we are all in deep, deep trouble.

In the last couple of weeks I have had the chance to ask three different people from the same state agency a question that affects a lot of sportsmen. From these three different people, all in law enforcement, I received three different answers to the same question. I surely hope this makes them only half as bad as the IRS, but I do have to wonder how in the world they expect the average party out in the woods to know what to do and how to behave!

I still say even after all the people I have run into in my travels, that way over 90% of the people out there in the woods want to do right. But, they do have to know what right is. It used to be that people could be told, as I was told at least a zillion times in growing up, just use the thing on your shoulders that God gave you. In other words use your head and good old common sense. But, one has to really stop and think, and then wonder if good old common sense will work in the '90's. I, for one, am not sure it will.

It must really be hard on a father now that takes his kids out to do something and he cannot even tell them right from wrong, because it changes so often. You may not believe this, but when I first started working as a conservation officer, about 99% of the tickets you wrote were out of three-four paragraphs or sections of all the laws. Now you can have subjects that we are suppose to know about with sections in any number of different laws.

Let me explain something. Here sits one of our legislators down in the "Big House". There is really nothing going on today so he gets reading some of his mail. In his mail he finds a number of letters from a special interest group trying to get one of their special projects approved or disapproved. The legislator is in a close race so gets thinking, just maybe something should get done about this to get them in my corner. So about 2:00am a bill is being worked on to legalize dog racing down in Detroit. This bill has a real good chance of passing so our legislator from up north gets his bill affecting what we may do out in the woods attached to this Detroit dog racing bill and they both pass. So here is a bill governing what can be done with something in the U.P. under a dog-racing bill for Detroit. When this happens you can have pieces of laws all over the books instead of all the game laws under an Act titled *The Game Act of 19--*, or all the fishing laws under *The Sports Fishing Act of 19--*. There are just too many back-door laws on the books in this day and age!

And we are suppose too know this when we go out in the field?

But the best may be yet to come. You see after this law is passed, the agency that has the duty to enforce it, takes the law and sits down with it and decides what it says or tries to interpret what this legislator meant when he wrote it. Right here you know we are all in trouble on account of all the Expsurts involved in this part of the process.

Back in the good old days every officer in the field got a draft of all laws that were in the system that may affect what he was enforcing out in the woods. The officer could then read them over, talk to some local sportsmen groups, and have a chance to respond to the laws before they were passed. This way everybody could have an input in the system.

I have to wonder if we would really be better off if we just paid our legislators to spend all their time away from the *Big House.* If they are not there they can do us no more harm. I could never be a legislator because I would have to operate and live by the principles I believe in, I could not change every time the wind changes directions. A prize example of this is where there is a need for an increase in the fees charged for hunting and fishing license. There is a plan put forth and the facts laid out from the opening of the session, but it is an election year so let's just sit on it. But, right after the election is over, during the end of November or early December session, the bill gets passed! Surprise! No, but I think the way the game is played the voters ought to be able to call a penalty for *un-sportsman*-like conduct! If we could, maybe things would change. Well, I hope you have read your digest and the page of law changes and understand them all. If you are lucky enough to, just maybe you will make it through the fall without any problems.

My Opinion-3
I have to ask whose idea was this?

There are very few people in this world that are as lucky as I have been. To have had the job I did and then being able to retire before hitting fifty, what more could a guy ask for. When you are this lucky after retiring you get to spend time almost every day from the opening of hunting season till it closes out in the woods. When you spend this much time out in the woods you may just learn a few things. The funny thing is that after I retired I get to spend even more time out in the woods then I did while working as a game warden. Believe this? You have to remember all the meetings, court time, paper work, etc. that the officers have to put up with. After many heart-breaking hours spent thinking about it, I figured I could live and enjoy life a lot more without all these things.

Well, at least after today we can see and hear something besides what we have had to listen to! (*After the November elections and all the election ads were over*) Maybe the good Lord gives us the great outdoors just so we can have a place to retreat to with no TV, no radios, no papers, just the peace and quiet to enjoy. Do you ever really need this? Sometimes I do. I can walk through the woods with my dog, stop and sit on a log for a while, pet the dog and really have peace of mind. Sometimes when you do this all the other things you usually wonder and worry about just seem a little farther off.

Well, how many kids are going to make it home this year? Do you realize that by the time next week's paper is out we will be into the real hunting season! This is a prediction from an old man that spends almost every afternoon out in the woods, except Sunday. There are just not the deer in a lot of areas this year as the last couple. Besides what I observe, I talk to a lot of people and most of them say the same thing. There are a few areas that are reporting good numbers of deer, but its not up north. Don't get me wrong, there are deer out there and it should be a good season, but get ready...

One thing that bothers me that I have to say something about is the mess with Antler-less deer permits. I have to ask myself, "Self? How many deer does one person need?" "Is it a trailer load?"

Don't get me wrong, I see nothing the matter with a party taking a couple deer if the family will make use of them. But! I have a real problem with those that want to get half a dozen permits just to see how many they can shoot. I always tell people, "There is a difference between a hunter and a shooter. The hunter is our old type sportsman that loves the outdoors, likes seeing and watching and enjoying things, plus also likes to take a deer or two that the family will use before the next hunting season rolls around. The shooter is the person that has to take as many as they can get away with or else they feel they did not have a good hunting season. It is wrong!"

What bothers me is the fact that I feel that the *Exspurts* down in the "Big House" are making a mistake here in what they are teaching young hunters. First of all, the landowner's permits are called landowner's permits. Now, even a guy that grew up in Ontonagon can figure out that if something says a landowner's permit, it should be for the landowner. But under the way they do things it is not. It is basically for anyone and everyone the landowner wants to give his tax ID number to. The other thing is that these landowner permits are for deer to be shot on the land or adjacent to the land the permit is for. Give me a break! There is not one out of ten that are used this way. Once a deer is shot and hanging up or even in the back of a pickup how is an officer ever going to be able to tell where it was shot at to control these permits? On top of these out of control landowner's permits, throw the famous block permits that are also uncontrollable. But, then you can always blame the change in the deer herd on old man winter in your area.

Now, don't misunderstand me. I have no problem with antler-less deer permits, but I do have a problem with wholesale meat hunters permits. I'm sorry, but I was just not raised this way even if I was raised in the U. P.

Remember to check things out before you head out next week. If you use a boat make sure all the safety equipment is in it. If you are going to try to cross the old beaver pond or creek on the ice make sure about the ice. Check out the gas stove and frig at camp. Check your firearm each and every time you handle it, before and during the season. Learn to do it so often it just becomes a habit. No loaded guns in camp. Respect the rights of others and remember that those of us that use a deer blind are being watch by big brother this year to see how we behave. Let's not blow it.

I always tell the youth at hunter safety, "Remember that those people that a person hunts with are always there family or friends, so usually if you allow an accident to happen it is usually someone you love that gets hurt."

Have a safe hunting season. And grandpa let the kids or grandkids pull out the big one you get for you.

My Opinion-4
I would never have thought this could ever happen

This falls under, *"Don't say I didn't warn you when you told me it could never happen!"*

One thing about writing my books is the fact I have got on a number of mailing lists for outdoor papers and newsletters. I received one this week that should scare us all. We all have our opinion of the vote coming up next month on bear hunting. The hunters and the people that are for wise wildlife management say this is just the start of some people trying to end hunting in this country. Others laugh and say you are overreacting. But! Listen to this!

In an out-of-state sportsman's paper I receive weekly, there was this article where a number of people had got together and bought an old abandoned farm. There were no buildings left on the land and it was pretty well grown over. All they wanted to use this land for was as a place to get away, do a little camping with the kids, and some hunting in the fall of the year. It looked like a perfect place where they owned a couple hundred acres of their own and would not be closed in by someone right next to them.

They did not want to live there so they just made a few places to park their trailers or pop-up campers for a few days. It was a dream come true with the woods and enough land to wander around on and just enjoy. But, there were those that did not want them to enjoy it so they started out to put a stop to it. Why? I have no idea and for the life of me cannot think of any that would make any sense. When it got to the point where they had to come up with an ingenious way to stop these criminals from camping on the land they owned and paid taxes on they had a method to their madness. They looked in the zoning laws and found that the land in this part of the county, even the old farm land that had not been farmed in years, was zoned agriculture. Under the definition of agriculture land in the zoning laws it did not cover someone coming in for the weekend and parking a camper and walking around in the now wild land they owned. It did not cover using the land for hunting and maybe a zillion other things.

A trial found the new owners not guilty of improper use of the old farm land, but the people that wanted to stop them then went back and found a law out of the 1930's and used this to get all this criminal activity stopped on this old farm. The case has now worked its way all the way up to the top court of that state. Crazy? Yes, but this seems to be the way our nation is going now. Are my rights being taken away important to you? Yes! Because yours may be next. Don't ever say, *"But that could never happen here in our country!"* It already did for a lot of other people.

I guess the older I get the more confused I get. As I have said before, there are just too many laws out there and too many courts out there making new laws out of laws that were never meant to be used this way when they were written years and years ago. Are we or will we be better off with all these new ideas and laws? I don't really think so. In this old gray-headed guy's mind we will be sorry we ever did some of the things we do down the road someday. The ones I really feel sorry for are our kids and grandkids, who will have to live with all the dumb things this new found generation has done to remove all the old landmarks our forefathers placed there to protect us, not stop us from doing what was right.

I tell my family, life is tough now, years ago a man could saddle his horse when government got out of control, and ride west till he got out where there was none. Then he could start over and it would be years before all those Exspurts with their new found wisdom would get out where he was to mess things up. We can't do this now; we are just stuck with this mess.

Some of the Theiler crew out in front of camp

*What a hunting shack, if only all the tales told
here had been written down. (Look at the rifles next to the Door)*

Chapter 10

Conservation Officer's Stories
Upper Michigan Tales from a Game Warden's Perspective

Hunters

Hunters Notes

Well, I guess if you have hunted deer most of your life and then get around to hunting bear there is quite a change in how it is done. When you take the habits of these two animals and compare them, what a surprise. In all my travels through the woods I can count on my fingers how many bear I have ever observed. You just do not see them moving about too often. The other thing people do not seem to realize is the fact that a bear, when moving through the woods, does not make a sound unless it wants to. The other thing you soon realize is how silly people are about Michigan black bear. We will get into this some other time.

I first want to thank all the people, both hunters and non-hunters, that helped us protect the right to harvest bear here in Michigan. I think all of us were surprised by the percentage of voters that voted to allow us to enjoy our time spent out in the outdoors trying to take a bear. This following article is one I wrote after the November ('96) vote took place that I feel in my heart tells the truth.

A Wake Up Call

This past November a ton of money was spent trying to convince the voters of Michigan the pros and cons of bear hunting in Michigan, as we know it. I, for one, am sure glad that the voters of Michigan saw through some of the things that were being said and voted to continue bear hunting here in our state. But! I do not think it was a vote in favor of the way some people behave and do things!

First before I get started let me say something else. When you stop and think about it, it a crying shame all the money that was spent on both sides of this issue that could have been used to further so many needed conservation programs. Now I realize that once this matter got started there was no choice but for those involved to team together and fight for their right to hunt. But stop and think of how much could have been done with all this money if not for a very few hunters. How much wetland habitat could have been purchased or improve, or deer yarding areas? How many studies that are always needing more money to find out things to benefit us all could have completed their work? You could go on and on thinking about what could have been.

Now to get back to the cause of this vote.

In my travels around the state with my books, I talk to hundreds and hundreds of outdoor people. During these conversations I heard this statement over and over, "If the vote was just to stop dog-bear hunting I think I may have voted in favor of it, but seeing what they were really trying to do, I vote against it." When you get so many people making the same statement just maybe we had better stop and think about it.

How come you can have some dog-bear hunters that you never hear about? (And there are some in our area.) While with others it seems like every time they hit the woods they make somebody else mad at bear hunters. There is no doubt in my mind that it has to be the attitude of the crew of hunters. One party has the character to respect the rights and property of others; while the other party says in the way they operate *"stick it in your ear! I'm going to do what I want and there is nothing you can do about it!"* Well, for years they have gotten away with this attitude. The only thing is the way this small percentage of bear-dog hunters operate almost cost all hunters their right to hunt.

I say hunt, because if it had passed to outlaw bear hunting as we know it, there is no doubt in this person's mind it would have only been a sign of things to come.

What should all of us learn from things that took place last fall? I think it is up to us as hunters to clean up our act. When you are attending a sportsman's club meeting or an annual convention of an organization you may belong to and someone starts telling a tale where they infringed on someone else's rights, or circumvented the law so they could do what they wanted, tell them they were wrong. I think for too many years the rest of us hunters have kept silent or acted like it didn't bother us, when it always has. I feel the true hunter that loves the outdoors and enjoys his hunting and fishing had better let himself be heard. Stand up against those that think they are being cute, tell them they are being a "jerk", and if they don't stop it we are all going to someday pay for their actions!

I hear over and over in my travels since this vote, "Boy, we sure taught those anti-hunting people a lesson!" No! Even if you may be right, we, too, should learn a lesson from what has happened, and if we let it happen again it is our own fault.

Let me ask you something, how many new deer blinds were taken into the woods and left even after all that took place over the use of deer blinds? How dumb can we as hunters be after the debate on this issue? How many hunters still caused problems while baiting even after the hearings? (Thank goodness most of the stories I heard were not from our area.)

How many chances do we need as hunters to do things right before we wake up some day and we cannot do it at all? Even after all the articles I have written, it is hard sometimes to put into words what you observe taking place, and hope and pray that the day will not come when some of us will have to say, "I told you so, you sure were warned enough about it, you have nothing to complain about now, it's too late now anyway."

Hey Buddy! That's My Apple!

Fawn That Moved Into My Blind!

Chapter 11

Conservation Officer's Stories

Upper Michigan Tales from a Game Warden's
Perspective

Justice

Well, I guess this tale could fall under the category, *"Justice Prevails!"*

It seems that there was this deer hunter that had not been at it very long, but liked the idea of getting away from things and being out in the woods. On this morning he left home before daylight to make his way to his hunting area. But, he mis-con-figrated and daylight did arrive even before he got to his hunting area.

As he drove along right after daylight he also found out that he was not the only one that knew about this perfect hunting area, because there was this other pickup right in front of him. Seeing it was already daylight, he slowed down and let this other pickup get a ways in front of him.

Would you believe it! As he drove slowly along this back road on his way to his hunting spot he got himself a deer! But what now! This was always in his plan, but he had never really expected to get one, so he did not really know what to do next. But he was lucky enough to know where some buddies were hunting so he went to find them for some help.

When they returned together to take care of his deer, they found it was gone. He felt it sure had not went off by itself, because he was sure it was dead, and after all he had supposedly tagged it. This crew got thinking and our almost a hunter remembered the pickup that had been in front of him. Just maybe...

With the aid of one of those car-phones they called to see if there was a game warden in the area that could help them out. Would you believe it! There was! The officer came out and the hunter told him about getting a deer and then going for help, only to return to find his deer gone. The officer, with the hunters following, decided to follow the two-track to the area of some camps to see if just maybe they could find this other pickup and the lost deer.

Sure enough after a short drive they came to this camp with a couple pickups parked in front of it. One was a newer type pickup with one of these fiberglass shells on the back just like the hunter had told the officer he had followed right after daylight. The officer pulled up in front of the camp and was met by a number of men that came out of the cabin.

This officer explained to this crew what had happened down the road and the fact they were looking for this hunter's deer. Our crew from the camp claimed to know nothing about any deer and in fact had not even got out hunting yet this morning. No, matter what question was asked the answer was always the same, "No, we have yet to even get a deer here at camp."

Well, it seemed like maybe this had been a wild goose chase, so the officer talked to them a few minutes and was about ready to leave when all of a sudden there was a loud crash and the sound of breaking glass!!! Then some more pounding and more sounds of glass and items breaking. This whole crew standing there, (the officer, the hunter and his buddies, and the crew from the camp) all looked over at this new pickup with the fiberglass shell just in time to see the leg of a deer come out through the side of this fiberglass shell once again!!!

It seems that our dead deer, that wasn't even there, had suddenly remembered that he wasn't that dead after all! After totally wrecking this parties pickup shell while kicking around in it, our deer finally remembered he was supposed to be dead, so he returned to that state.

The moral of the tale is; our first guy, the real hunter got his deer back. Our second guy not only no longer had a shell for his new pickup, but also now found himself with a ticket from the officer for having the deer. But, only "You Know Who" really knows when our deer really made that final big jump into the far beyond, was it before or after getting even with the guy trying to fudge and steal him from this other hunter?

But Officer, It's Not Polite to Laugh

I guess one of the most frustrating times of an officer's career is when he is trying to stop an ORV that is just not going to stop, no matter what! I don't care what the officer does; this party just keeps on going. What is the officer going to do?

I know what he would like to do! Reach down and pull out the carbine and try for the motorcycle taking off across the field for target practice! But he can't, so he usually arrives at the point where he has to quit and only hopes there will be another day. This was one of those days.

On this weekend afternoon another officer and myself were working in a state game area where motorcycles were wrecking the state land. They had worn away all the vegetation and topsoil so that there were big ditches throughout the area made from the runoff after a heavy rain.

These state game areas were purchased from taxes hunters pay on the sporting goods they purchase. It is through a federal program under what is called the Pitman-Roberts Act. When this land is purchased with this money it is to be used for wildlife management programs. For this reason, it's illegal for ORV's to be tearing it up.

While working the hill country down near Millington, in the Thumb area of Michigan, we observed a number of motorcycles. We tried to head off this one biker on a dirt bike, but there was no way we could get him to stop without someone getting hurt. This rider was going so fast and reckless that there was no way we were ever going to get him to stop. After trying a number of times to get ahead of him, so we could block his way, we gave up and went to check out some other trails.

A little while later we came back through this same area in our travels and observed a car coming across a field with the trunk open on it. We parked out near the edge of the road and let it come to us. As they pulled up on the road we walked back to the car to see just what they had in the trunk, and would you believe it!

Here in the trunk lay what was left of the motorcycle we had been trying to catch a few hours earlier. To this day we never found out what he hit, but needless to say the motorcycle was now in enough pieces and small enough to fit in the trunk of their car. Once again, justice had evened out the score.

Yooper Laser Sight

Grandpa Theiler, who I learned to tell stories from and his hunting crew (Top Left)

A Yooper's successful hunt

Chapter 12
Conservation Officer's Stories
Upper Michigan Tales from a Game Warden's Perspective
Yooper Butcher

As you well know, some of my favorite people are the so-called Exspurts. For some strange reason, when this fact became known with the publishing of my books you would be amazed what comes my way. Here is one piece of scientific literature and some true Yooper wisdom.

Venison vs Beef

The Taste Controversy Ends
United State Venison Council

Controversy has long raged about the relative quality and taste of venison and beef as gourmet foods. Some people say that venison is tough, with a strong, wild taste. While others insist that the flavor is delicate.

An Independent food research group was retained by the United States Venison Council to conduct a taste test to determine the truth of these conflicting assertions.

First, a grade-A-choice Holstein steer was chased into a swamp a mile and a half from the nearest road and shot several times. The holes were anywhere between the head and tail. After some of the entrails (for you Yoopers, guts) were removed, the carcass was dragged over rocks and logs, and through mud and dirt. Then thrown into the back of a pickup truck, covered with chain saw gas and oil, transported through rain and snow for 100 miles before being hung in the sun for 10 days to help provide suet to all the birds around the area.

After that it was lugged into the garage, where it was skinned, while being rolled around on the garage floor for a while. After going over the carcass with a folded up, burning newspaper to remove the excess hair, strict sanitary precautions were observed throughout this test, within the normal limitations of a Yooper's butchering environment.

For instance, dogs and cats that tried to sniff the steer's carcass were quickly chased out of the garage if they attempted to lick the carcass or bite hunks out of it!

Next a sheet of plywood left out in the back yard to be cleaned off by nature from last years butchering, was set up in the basement on two saw horses. The pieces of dried blood, meat and fat left from last year were scraped off with the wire brush from the tool box, last used to clean out the dry grass that plugged up the grass shoot under the riding lawnmower.

The skinned carcass is then dragged down the steps leading from the garage to the basement so a half dozen inexperienced, but enthusiastic, people can work on it with meat saws, cleavers, and dull knives. The results were 375 pounds of soup bones, four bushel baskets of meat scraps, and a couple of steaks that were an eighth of an inch thick on one edge, and an inch and a half thick on the other edge.

The steaks were then seared on a glowing red, cast iron frying pan, to lock in the flavor quickly. When the smoke cleared, rancid bacon grease was added along with three pounds of onions, and the whole conglomeration fried for two hours.

The meat was then gently scraped and teased from the frying pan with a paint scraper to be served to three blindfolded taste test panel volunteers. Every one of the members of the panel thought it was venison!

One taste test volunteer even went so far as to say, it tasted exactly like the venison he had eaten at hunting camp for the last twenty-seven years.

There, for the results of this trail showed conclusively that there is no difference at all between the taste of beef and venison to the average Yooper!

Wake Up Dad!

This is one of those tales that came to me from a reader of my books. It is one of those stories, where, if Dad lives to be a hundred years old he still will never live it down.

It seems that there was this father and son that went out deer hunting together. In the area where they liked to hunt there were a number of high ridges, but it was a really a good deer area.

On this nice, warm, sunny afternoon they had made plans for Dad to sit on one side of the ridge and his young son to sit across from him on another ridge, where, if anything happened he could always get Dad's attention.

After they had been sitting for a while, on this sunny afternoon, the son decided to take the pair of field glasses he had with him and check out how Dad was doing across on the other side of the ridge from him. As he looked the area over with the field glasses he soon spotted good, old Dad.

There he was sitting in the warm sunshine, with his back leaning against a tree, his deer rifle across his legs, sound asleep! He might have known, after all isn't this part of hunting.

All of a sudden while still looking through the field glasses he saw some movement a little farther on down the ridge, but right in front of Dad. He moved the field glasses over and sure enough here was a real nice buck standing down the ridge right in front of his Dad. As the boy watched, while Dad was still sound asleep, the buck took a couple of steps right towards where Dad was still sound asleep under the tree, dreaming of the big buck that was surely going to come his way.

By now, the boy could watch both the buck and his Dad in the field glasses at the same time. Slowly and steadily, the buck was working his way along the ridge closer and closer to where Dad slept under the tree. And here sat son to watch it all, but too far away to do anything about it.

As he watched, all of a sudden the buck stopped still, its ears went forward, his tail went up, he gave a loud snort, and bounded over the ridge!

Up flew his Dad off the ground, his deer rifle going to his shoulder as he swung to cover the area where the snort had come from! But you know it is hard to kill a deer by shooting it in the snort!

What a time could be had if only this had happened in the day and age of the video cameras.

Rob's big buck, he had a smile then!

Chapter 13

Conservation Officer's Stories
Upper Michigan Tales from a Game Warden's Perspective

O'Goody Another Vacation

Well, I guess all fathers have traveled through one of those family vacations that will live forever in family history. I have been on a few as the stories in some of my books attest to. I have also been where things took place that makes me think that other fathers may have been there too.

Our Vacation

One day while I was traveling down a six-lane highway, I observed a station wagon loaded with kids parked along the edge of the road. As they sat there, here was the dad out re-tying all the gear that was on top of their car. There was no doubt in my mind that this was another family heading north on another of those family vacations.

Now, first of all you have to understand that in order to qualify to go on one these family vacations you have to own a mini van or station wagon with a trailer hitch and a car top carrier. You also must have a minimum of four kids in your family, but the more the better. Also this must be one of those vacations where you are trying to include a little something for everybody to personally enjoy.

The first step on this vacation is to get ready and pack the vehicle. This is why you need at least a mini-van with a trailer attached and a car top carrier. You see you have to take 99% percent of everything you own, so just in case you need it you will have it with you.

Checklists:

(1) Clothes and personal needs for six people. Play clothes, Sunday clothes, swimming clothes, hiking clothes, warm clothes, cool clothes, rain clothes. Plus personal needs, this means a minimum of twelve suitcases before you even start to pack. Top this off by at least thirty-seven pairs of shoes to cover all these clothing needs and activities.

(2) Then there are the sporting goods you need for this trip up north. There are six mountain bikes, all the fishing gear for everybody, the tennis rackets, the ball gloves and bats, roller- blades, dad's guns so he can get a little practice in. This means also shells, clay pigeons and thrower, targets, and ear protection. Do we include here mom's cross stitch items and all the books she is going to read while everybody else is going about their activity?

(3) Then the camping gear: There is the tent large enough to hold six people or so they say. The Coleman stove, five cans of gas, three Coleman lights, two bug lights, six air mattresses and six sleeping bags, ten pillows, ground tarp and one to throw over the tent after it is set up. There are also ten-gallon water jugs to hold store- bought water for these city folks. In addition, there is enough food to last for ten days because they can save $2.10 if they purchase it at a BIG store downstate where they can save all this money. There are also three Teddy Bears, six dolls with all their clothes, and the two family dogs that fall in this area with their two bags of dog food seeing they will not both eat the same brand.

Now, with all this stuff sitting out in front of the garage, you are ready to load up for the family vacation. O' goody!

One of the keys to doing this right is to go and purchase a pack of this cheap nylon rope that we have all bought. It is the type rope where you purchase 50 feet of rope and by the time you return home you have at least 75 or 100 feet of rope, it has stretched that much.

You finally get everything loaded and pry everybody into the car and off you go. A few hours later here you sit along the expressway re-tying things as I go by.

About a half mile farther along the expressway, behind the father repacking everything on top his vehicle, I observe a brand new tent, still in the box, lying in the center lane of the expressway. The tent poles were still sticking out of the box from where dad placed them after making sure the tent was large enough and would be easy to set up.

As of yet it had not been run over, but this did not take long to happen on this busy expressway. I don't think our dad back up the expressway had the slightest idea that he had lost anything when the items on top the car worked loose. Guys have you ever been there?

er dark you finally pull into Indian Lake State Park. The kids are about as helpful as a hurt female bear after being cooped up in a ar all day. The dogs are both a basket case. So then you are ready ing your campsite, to just get the tent set up. Then take out some nom can fix supper, so you can sit down and just relax, to start ation.

pull all the gear off the top of the station wagon and look for the tent. And you look! And you look! But you cannot find any sign of the tent! It is just not there and you are sure you packed it, you are at least sure of that.

You look at wifee who is also looking for the tent by now, and you are saying, "I know I packed it, I remember putting it on top the car." So he hears from wifee, "If you had packed it, it would be here!"

"But Honey, I can remember getting it out of the shed and putting it with the camping gear we were going to take, honest honey, I did not forget to pack it."

"You must have, we both can see that it is not here!"

"Well, I don't know what could have happened to it, but I can picture in my mind placing it on top the car with the other camping gear. But I did hear that in some state parks you can rent a tent to use for camping"

I could never figure out why state parks would bother to rent tents until I saw this tent lying in the middle of the expressway.

It's to save the husband's life just in case he should ever run into anything like this vacation.

Hubby Does It Again

This could only happen to a true Yooper husband.

There was this party that had to come to town to attend a funeral. He got ready to go and decided to drive to where his wife worked so they could both ride together. When he got there they decided to take her car and leave his truck at the place where she worked.

They both went to the service at the funeral home and after this was over the husband decided to go out to the graveside service at the cemetery. The wife said she would just walk back to where she worked; it was only a couple of blocks away. So hubby took her car and went out to the cemetery.

After the graveside service the husband walked around for a minute or two, then made his way back to his wife's car to head back to town. He got the keys out and got in the vehicle all ready to return to town. As he tried to start the car the key would not turn in the ignition. We all have known these new cars with the locking steering column, where you had to wiggle the steering wheel a little to get the key to turn. He tried all this with no luck.

This car, his wife's, had one of those buttons on the steering column you pushed to get the key out, so he played with this thinking something was wrong here. No luck, the key would fit in, but just would not turn. By this time he was at the cemetery all by himself, out in the country, except for the man from the funeral home who had not left yet. This man came over and they both played with trying to get the key to turn in the ignition. No luck. It would move a little, but just would not turn. Wiggle this, push that, monkey with this, no luck the key would just not turn.

Finally it was decided he would hitch a ride back to town in the hearse. But, he figured that this uncooperative car belonging to his wife could just sit there with the keys in it. Just maybe someone will come along and steal it! So off they went heading back to town.

The hearse driver swung by where his wife worked and dropped him off so he could get his pickup. He then planed on finding someone to go out and help him figure out what was wrong with the wife's car. Out he got and walked across the street to get his truck, reaching into his pocket to get the truck keys out.

Truck Keys! Truckkeys! Truck..........

As a light bulb seemed to light up in his head!

As he took the _Truck_ keys out of his pocket, he realized they were his wife's car keys! Both the car and truck were the same makes. Now he knew why the key back out in his wife's car at the cemetery would not turn in the ignition of her car! Almost, but not quite!

Here my buddy now stands, in town, next to his truck, with the wife's car keys! But his truck key, for the truck he is now standing by, are miles away out at the cemetery in the ignition of his wife's car he had left there.

This just goes to prove once again that, "Two wrongs do not make a right."

My Dad on his awesome snowmachine
(You should have seen the one before this!

Author

Chapter 14
Conservation Officer's Stories
Upper Michigan Tales from a Game Warden's Perspective
Game Warden's Wisdom

A Retired Yooper Game Warden's Perspective on Life

I guess we have all had things happen to us that just make us stop and wonder at times. When this happens I have to wonder if we always give credit where credit is due. Sometimes we plan things out with our normal Yooper wisdom (There is one example here) while other times just maybe the Real Planner is better at it then we are.

These next couple of items fall under the category of strange but true. I have always said that the good Lord cares about the little things that make us happy.

Who do you think planned these?
A Christmas Gift

There were some parents (who I knew from back in Ontonagon) that ask their son what he would like for Christmas. He is an avid outdoors person, so he told them about a pair of really nice gloves he would like. After the parents checked on them, they told their son that there was just no way they could get them for him this year at what they cost.

A week or so later this Mom and Dad were on their way to one of the larger cities in the U.P. and as I said before, if you are planning on traveling it will surely snow. On this day it was really snowing, in fact, in places it was like two-track driving. As they went along, they came to an area where a snowplow had made a pass down one side of the road. While traveling slowly along on account of the road conditions, they observed a glove lying in the road.

Now all good Yoopers have at least half-dozen sets of one glove only that they picked up in the road. In fact, it seems they are always for the same hand. (Twelve left-handed gloves laying around the garage and nothing to go on the right hand, unless you can make a left-handed glove fit on your right hand.) As Dad drove by the glove he asked his wife if she thought he should stop and pick it up. Finally, being a normal Yooper, he turned around and went back to pick it up.

As he got out to pick up this lone glove they had observed laying in the road, he looked over in the snow bank and saw part of what ended up being the other glove. Not only had he hit the Mother Load, two gloves for different hands, as they looked the gloves over they saw they were exactly the same type gloves their son had asked for, for Christmas. And the price was right.

Memories of Dad

Just before Christmas one year, while being my normal Mr. Clean, I went to throw some trash into a trash can in a public building. Lying on top the trash can was a cassette tape. Out of curiosity I picked the tape up. I figured it was either wrecked or one of those teenage tapes that are on a different wavelength and frequency than this old man's ears are used to. But, to my surprise, it seemed like a perfectly good tape.

I looked at the names of some of the songs on it and could not believe it! One of the first ones I noticed was one my Dad used to sing to us kids titled, *It No Secret What God Can Do*. There were also a number of others on this tape that were my Dad's favorites. I took this tape and headed for my car to see if it was any good. Sure enough, it was in perfect shape.

A chance happening? Or is there Someone that knows something that can be special to us and just lets it happen at times?

By Chance?

This past weekend wifee and I took three college-bound girls from town down to Madison, so they could make connections with another girl for their trip back to college. Saturday morning as the four girls were getting ready, I went out to sweep off their car for them. As I walked around the car, I noticed something was missing. The air from the passenger side front tire!

I went back into the house and told my boy Rob, "Get dressed there is a flat tire on the girl's car." As they came to put the rest of their baggage in the car I told them to take their time with breakfast because there was a flat tire on their car. Rob and I took it off and headed down for the tire shop where he has most of his work done. As we were going there he made the statement, "Nothing will be open this early in the morning." As we pulled into the parking lot two of the workers were just walking across to the garage. When they saw us, they said that they were not open yet. We told them we just wanted a flat fixed. They said if we had the exact amount they would do it for us. (They had no change yet in their money drawer.)

The first thing they noticed was that the valve stem was leaking, so they replaced it. They looked the tire over, checked the air pressure and off we went. When I was getting it out of the back of the pickup, Rob thought he heard something. Upon checking we found another small air leak and went back to get this fixed.

Do you think it was an accident, that this happened in my boy's driveway where we could get it fixed, instead of in the middle of nowhere between Madison and Pensacola, FL where the four girls were heading? I guess I like to think that "Someone" was looking out for these college-bound girls.

The key to a good life; learn to enjoy the little things that come along in life and give credit where credit is due.

Now, our true Yooper wisdom (When we are in charge)

If you live up here in God's country, in the great north woods, there are still a good number of people that heat their homes during the cold winter months with wood. If you do this, one of the most important things you have to remember to do is to clean out your chimney. If you should forget to do this you can be sure your wife will remind you about it.

There was this party living up here that decided that it was time to check out his chimney. The house he lived in was one of those chalet types where the roof comes down near the ground and is real steep. Seeing this was his first time working at this project he had to figure out just how to do it.

First, he placed a ladder on the far side of the house, and then he threw a heavy rope over the top of the roof and fastened it to a heavy object down on the ground. This project took a lot of figuring out, because when he got this done this time, it would make an even once he had accomplished it.

Now everything was set and he headed up the ladder with his chimney brush and other equipment in hand. When he got up to the chimney, which sat about a third of the way down the roof from the peak, he tied himself off with the heavy rope. Our chimneysweeper was just getting started and things were falling into place rather well. Just as he had planned. The rope was tied around his waist to hold him on the roof next to the chimney, so he was hid from anyone on the far side of the house.

His project was going along rather well, when all of a sudden he heard a noise! It sounded like a car door slamming! A sound he surely was not too interested in hearing right at this moment! He dropped his brush, grabbed the rope, and worked his way as fast as he could trying to get up to the peak of the house, so he could look down into the yard on the other side of the house.

Just as his head cleared the peak of the house, he spotted his wife. There she was sitting in the heavy object he had fastened the other end of his rope to so he could stay up on the roof.

Before he could yell! The engine started and the heavy object headed down the driveway as our chimneysweeper yelled for all he was worth. Which wasn't too much right at this moment. That is, he yelled till the rope went tight and all the slack was taken up, then he took off up over the peak, down the other side, and then skipping along the driveway behind the car!

Thank goodness his wife observed this bouncing set of arms and legs coming down the driveway behind the car and stopped the car to check it out.

BVD's are cold!

If you are one of those people that planned to save big bucks back during the energy crises by putting in a wood stove you soon learned a few things. I guess one of the main things was wondering where all the money you saved went too.

The other was the strange sound you came to learn about and feared hearing. One of these sounds would bring a person out of a dead sleep. You could be lying in bed without a care in the world. All of a sudden it sounded like a freight train was going right through your house. In fact, you soon figured it was going right up your chimney!

Out of bed you flew, right away knowing you had a chimney fire going full speed ahead. Out of the house you would run after jumping into your tennis as you headed out the door. Up the ladder to the garage roof, then up the house roof to the chimney.

After getting there and watching the flames shooting out of the chimney, you would start throwing hands full of snow down the chimney until you had the fire put out. All this in the cold, blowing snow, in the middle of winter, in the U.P.

About the time you were sure the fire was out, and things were quieting down, you realized it was rather cold up on the roof, in the middle of winter, in only your BVD's and your tennis. It sure is amazing what a Yooper will do when his Wifee panics.

№ 1138   ORIGINAL

CITIZEN PARKING VIOLATION

| STATE | LICENSE NUMBER |
| TIME | MAKE OF AUTOMOBILE |

This is not a ticket, but if it were within my power, you would receive two.

Because of your Bull Headed, inconsiderate, feeble attempt at parking, you have taken enough room for a 20 mule team, 2 elephants, 1 goat, and a safari of pygmies from the African Interior.

The reason for giving you this is so that in the future you may think of someone else, other than yourself. Besides, I don't like domineering, egotistical or simple minded drivers and you probably fit into one of these categories.

I sign off wishing you an early transmission failure, (on the freeway at about 4:30 p.m.) Also, may the Fleas of a thousand camels infest your armpits.

WITH MY COMPLIMENTS

*My favorite ticket when someone blocked a road.
Then sit & watch people as they read it.*

Chapter 15

Conservation Officer's Stories
Upper Michigan Tales from a Game Warden's
Perspective

Clones

So what's new? Clones?

This defiantly falls under, "So what's new?"

I have to laugh when all of a sudden we are hearing all this news about the Exspurts *cloning* things! Ha!!! The people in Washington, Lansing, and 99% percent of the colleges have been trying to do it to people for years!

Why do you think the old time sayings like, "Use your head, that's what God placed it on your shoulders for." "Be an individual, use your head, if everybody else jumped off the Siphon Bridge, would you jump off it too?" "The first person to start one of these fads is a leader, the next ten thousand that follow after him are just followers!" "Where did all the common sense go?" There is just no end to all these questions the over 50 crowd heard while they were growing up.

For years we have passed laws to try and make everybody do the same thing, like the same thing, eat the same thing, wear the same thing, all cars now look alike, every thing now is *"Fat Free"* or is going to be or wants to be, gas can be from the Middle East, North Sea, or South America and when it gets to the pumps in Manistique it's all the same price, if you are a Detroit Lion fan you just have to get used to losing, while a Packer fan knew it was just a matter of time, "Why can't you get A's in school your sister gets A's,.......... and then we get mad at the poor sheep and monkey and call them a clone. I can't believe it.

We have all heard dozens of cases where kids in school have been in trouble because a law was passed to keep drugs and guns out of the school and someone brought an object or some medicine that fell into the *letter of the law* and some clone could not see the difference. Why does this happen, because we are no longer allowed to, *"Use your head."*

If you don't believe me just listen to the news. New rules for baiting coming along? Lets clone all hunters to do things just like I want everybody to do them! New laws or a rule for this or that, it's my way or no way!

Don't blame poor Dolly the sheep or monkeys; we humans who are supposed to be the smartest ones of the bunch have been trying cloning for years.

Just no Bucks!

I guess after you have spent the greatest part of your life out in the woods one of the funniest things you hear over and over is, "This has to be the worst deer season I ever saw!" But if you take a writer like myself that has all these stories about how each deer season went, I can prove how only a few years ago that "Worst season there ever was" took place. The following is one of the articles I wrote for the paper after one of those "Worst seasons."

Well, the regular firearm deer season is finally over and according to what I heard it has been one of the slowest I have ever heard of. You could sit out there for hours at a time and not even hear a single shot on the first day. They got a few real nice deer, but a lot of those that always see and get a lot of deer did not even see any. There were a lot of buck signs around in some areas, but the crazy weather made them act different then in most years.

After much deep study I have come up with four good, solid, scientific reasons why there were so few bucks spotted during this past hunting season. I observed between eighty and a hundred deer in my travels, but never saw an antler.

Reason number one: The acid rain we are all hearing about all the time on the news now days tend to dissolve the bucks antlers. Therefore from the time the antlers grow till firearm deer season rolls around this acid rain has dissolved the antlers down to nothing. So all you see is antlerless deer and you thought all this time that really big deer you saw was a doe.

Reason number two: The "Green House" problem has caused the bucks to start losing their antlers about two months earlier then usual now. When this happens by the time deer season rolls around the bucks have already lost their antlers and you will have a deer season just like the one we had this past year.

Reason number three: My bait pile became the home for single and unwed mothers and their kids. We seem to hear more and more about how many one parent homes there are now days. Now, take my word for it this past deer season adds proof to this fact. Some nights there would be up to fifteen deer having supper without the dad of the home being anywhere around.

Reason number four: I have always heard, from people that are suppose to know about things like this, that baldness comes from the mother's side of the family. In other words, if you boys grow up to be bald you can blame it on your Mom's genes. Now if this is true, it only stands to reason we are going through an era where the doe of our deer herds have all the domineering genes. Therefore, we are going through a time of bald bucks and it is all moms' fault.

Reason number five: It has to have been caused by Global Warming. If this is taking place, like they tell us it is. Then the deer are moving out of your area, which is no longer suitable for white tail deer and into an area that is. Therefore, you have to remember that with the ice age coming back as some Exspurts tell us, and Global Warming coming from the other direction, the magnetic fields that work on the brains of all wild animals out there has caused them to move out of the area where you are hunting. So if your good old spot is no longer producing you must be right in the middle of one of those magnetic fields. You will just have to move your blind out of that area into one that is not affected.

But even if you should get around all these good valid reasons for not getting a buck each and every year, I guess if you are not in the right spot at the right time you will just get skunked! But, all in all, it sure is fun to get out in the woods each fall.

Pictures of the Good Old Days
Grandpa Theiler's Hunting Crew

The Swamp crew out in front of camp

*Can you believe the 3 deer with racks
like this all gotten in one drive?*

Chapter 16
Conservation Officer's Stories
Upper Michigan Tales from a Game Warden's Perspective
A License for Living

A License just for Living

Seeing we are going to be getting cabin fever for six extra weeks I thought I would take a minute and bring up something that falls under strange, but true! These items' Eino and Teivo really have a problem with. In fact just maybe it would be better if we made a rule that after a person gets out of grade school they are no longer qualified for going to Washington or Lansing. If you stop and think about how we do things now compared to years ago when we just used common sense how can you argue with this? Here's an example of "Big House" wisdom.

First, let me say that while working with the state there was a general feeling that there was a force field around the state office buildings down in Lansing. To make things worse, there was within this force field a brain-sucking machine. Time after time you would see an absolutely squared away person transfer from out in the field down to the "Big House." Then, within a few short weeks, their ability to think and operate like a normal person had somehow left their body never to return. The funny thing is you can take a perfectly normal Yooper legislator and send him off to the "Big House" and the same thing happens. Could this be the reason term limits passed?

Example: Eino is traveling along on his 1947 home made snowmachine along a county road. He is heading over to see what Teivo is up to. So he travels down the county road and then cuts across on an unplowed two-track to get to Teivo's house. But do you believe it as he comes up to Teivo's driveway he gets stopped by the local warden. No problem as he gets asked for his snowmobile registration, he has it and the stickers are on the machine. But then he gets asked, "Where is your trail permit?" Eino replies, "Trail permit? I have never operated on one of the snowmobile trails in my life! In fact the nearest groomed snowmobile trail is more than ten miles away from here!" Eino is then informed that this makes no difference. If he never uses a snowmobile on a groomed trail or not. If you own a snowmobile and plan to ride it, you have to purchase a trail permit to ride your snowmachine off your own land!

Now I ask you, would any legislator in their right mind ever let a law like this get passed? How in the world can you require a person to buy a license for something they never do, for something they never use? This could be a really dangerous precedent! I can see it now...

The revenue from fishing licenses drops way off and the DNR has a few more programs they would like to start... So what do they do, they talk to a few of these same legislators that passed this snowmobile trail permit bill. Lets see, there are fewer fishermen out there each year, but the health people tell us that eating fish is good for your health, so people are going to eat fish. Just maybe we ought to rewrite the law as far as requiring a fishing license goes.

Now lets see, now lets see, we can make it so you need a license to fish for, possess, or eat fish within the state of Michigan. It sounds fair, right? Of course, by the time these same legislators get done wifee and I would be in trouble again. If we wanted to go out to Tyelene's Restaurant for their Friday night fish fry, we would have to first stop at Foxey's Den to purchase a fishing license in order to eat fish. Or the butcher's new job at Ken's Fairway would be checking fishing licenses before you can purchase any seafood products.

You people that are out there riding your snowmachines even if you never use a snowmobile trail, be careful! I was watching a piece on TV the other night where the DNR was complaining because they were not getting enough revenue from the trail permits. So the word is out to get you that do not have one. The poor trail grooming program is running short of money.

I bet you cannot comprehend that Eino thinks this is a stupid, unconstitutional, piece of legislation! How can you require a person to purchase a license or permit for something they do not use or do? Maybe some judge with a backbone should let the people in the "Big House" know this.

Well, I ran out of room, but if you want to keep going check on the newer, easier, income tax law that was passed at the other "Big House" in

Washington last year. I have to wonder where we would be today if Ben Franklin had needed all the permits and licenses of today to fly his kite? Lets see, an electrician's license, a locksmith license, an..............

What's the difference between a license and a fee?

This week I have come across a few items that really get Eino and Teivo going. The Forestry Division has found their crying towel about the fact that the legislator has not passed the 'Picken & Plucken' bill they want. One of the larger U.P. newspapers did a big article on this fact a while back.

I also wrote about it before, where there are those that would like to see the day come where whenever or whatever we do on either state or federal land you would pay a fee for doing it. I personally think it is time to dump some more tea into Manistique Harbor or wherever it was that our forefathers dumped the tea!

Now this is a trick question for you from the Big House where Eino has been studying this modern math from our legislators. You see, I have often wondered where all these ideas and changes of the math system came from, now I know.

You also see, Democrats call it a tax when they take another $20.00 bill out of your pockets for one of their pet projects. But Eino tells me that Republicans don't like taxes and cam-pain to cut them, so they do not raise your taxes like the Democrats. They just call everything a fee, users' fee, this fee, that fee, etc.

In fact, their programs gave Teivo a new verse to the old song they used to sing in grade school. "Old McDonald had a farm with a fee, fee here and a fee, fee there and here a fee, there a fee, everywhere a fee, fee, old McDonald had a farm."

Now back to Eino's question and modern math. If the Democrats pass a tax that takes $20.00 out of your pocket or the Republicans pass a fee that takes $20.00 out of your pocket, what is the difference? Are we not in both cases out the $20.00?
Or, if they both have their way, $40.00?

But you have to remember with modern math two negatives make a positive, so somehow we should come out ahead with losing this $40.00. But somehow, even this backwoods lad born in Ontonagon seems to think that no matter what terms are used, a person still has less money in their pocket when the politicians get done.

It reminds me of a story I was told by a friend, another game warden, one time. It seems he purchased this pair of Easter Bunnies to arrive at their house on Easter. In the course of time these bunnies became a herd and seeing back in this day and age you usually had to use things to make ends meet, what better way then to make use of some rabbits. Mom and dad were to soon find out that there was no way their kids were going to be part of eating the Easter Bunny!! Mom fried it, mom baked it, and in fact mom barbecued it! Dad even went so far as to clean all the meat off the bones and grind it up for patties! But no matter what you did it was still the Easter Bunny! From every side and every angle the kids were smart enough to realize it was still the Easter Bunny and the kids would not think of eating the Easter Bunny!

Call it a fee, call it a tax, but are we as smart as the kids to see the Easter Bunny or not?

But Officer! I tried!

Did you ever wake up in the morning and wonder what more could be added to the shoulders of sportsmen? This story tries to cover what a normal, red blooded, Yooper sportsman has to put up with now.

It seems the Exspurts who could never make the point system work for waterfowl, now want to try it on deer! No matter how hard they tried, they ended up going back to a regular bag limit on ducks, so now they want us to count points on deer before we shoot! This is something I have never made it a point to do, count points that is.

Then if this doesn't make life hard and interesting enough they are coming up with early, late, special, permit deer seasons. Thank goodness there are none in our area yet. I suggest you pick up your hunting guide early so you can study it long before you ever enter the woods. For some reason, why does it seem its getting more and more like the *"easy"* IRS guide for our taxes?

Then maybe you had better find a lawyer buddy to hunt with so he can help you figure out all the licenses, seasons, and special hunting regulations. If he can't, all I can wish you is *"Good Luck."*

By the way, this falls under, *"Did you know?"* The card you now send in for a doe permit is no longer a permit to shoot an antlerless deer! It is now a permit to purchase _another_ license so you can shoot an antlerless deer.

Now let me see, a bear permit (1) that gives you the right to purchase a bear license if you are ever lucky enough to be successful in the drawing (2). Then a turkey permit, that gives you the right to purchase a turkey license (4). Then the doe permit (5) that gives you the right to purchase a doe license (6). A small game license (7).

Then there is the state duck stamp (8). This to go along with the federal waterfowl stamp (9).

Now a regular firearm deer license (10) to go along with your archery deer license (11). And at the time this was typed you could still get a second deer license (12). This so you could still walk around in the woods during firearm deer season if you wanted to carry that $700.00 rifle you only get to use a couple of weeks out of the year. Remember *"It's the law now"* that you have to be in possession of a valid kill tag to carry a rifle during deer season.

Then you can always take another gamble in life and try for an Elk permit (13). Don't worry you will never have to purchase this license. (14)

But while running around in the woods you may want to do a little trapping, so get a trapping license also (15).

Then remember the most worthless license there is here in the U.P. for another $16.00, an ORV sticker that you get absolutely nothing for. (16)

But maybe one of the greatest moves ever made by the legislator was already covered in this chapter up above, two licenses for your snowmachine (17)& (18).

O', you say you use a boat to get back where you hunt and camp? (19).

Also remember where and how to place your bow hunting scaffold (20) and now your firearm scaffold also with your name on them (21). Then make sure you have your name on your waterfowl blind (22) and your ground blind for deer hunting (23). Also remember your camping permit (24) and the trailer license for the trailer you use once a year deer season (25).

I'm sure I may have missed a few things that may have just fallen through the cracks, but after all you have to remember that I am more than fifty and it is hard to keep track of all these ever-changing things.

And if you are really lucky! Just maybe you have a wifee that hunts, along with a couple of kids. I mean we all want the great outdoors to help us raise our kids, right? But remember, if you have a youth that hunts there are a couple of licenses in the above they don't need, yet.

It really comes as no surprise in this day and age that they are placing computers in patrol cars with the conservation officers. You have to remember that things can get really complicated out there in the woods. What is really scary is the day may soon come that the average hunter will have to carry a laptop computer just to keep track of all the seasons, licenses, and permits he needs just to take a walk out in the woods.

I can just see it now as an officer walks into court with his computer printout.

"You see your Honor. This poor slob had license one through five. But was missing number six. Then he had seven through ten, but we could find no record on the computer about number eleven or twelve. But he did have thirteen and fourteen with him. But number sixteen is on another computer that I could not check today because it is down for re-programming. But your Honor he did tell me he had one but his brother used the snowmachine yesterday and had it in his pocket."

"Your Honor, seventeen through twenty-three seem to be in order as far as I can tell."

"O' by the way your Honor, this poor sucker forgot to wear his helmet while using his 4-wheeler to pick up some firewood on the forty he owns for hunting camp."

"Now about his wifee that was out there too...................."

You may as well just give the Judge your gun, ORV, boat and motor, camping trailer, your new pickup, and snowmachine and hope things come out even.

Now I ask you, is there any wonder that term limits were passed in Michigan? People are flat fed up with the way all this is going. I could also have listed at least three other licenses or permits that are already in the hopper at the state or federal level.

Sometimes I really think life is a joke, but for some reason I just do not feel like laughing about it.

How it used to be?

Could life get any better?

Chapter 17
Conservation Officer's Stories
Upper Michigan Tales from a Game Warden's
Perspective
Only A Hunter

This falls under, One That Got Away!

A young man told this to me ten years after the fact at an outdoor show. It seems that there were a couple of young guys out deer hunting. They had observed a few deer, but not any bucks. They had been hunting this area for bucks only because their doe permits were for another area about three miles west of where they were hunting.

After about the third day of hunting, while still seeing a lot of deer without antlers, the guy telling me this story, said he heard a shot over where his buddy was hunting. He worked his way over in that direction and sure enough his buddy had shot a deer. The only problem was this one did not have any antlers either!

He asked him, "Are you crazy! Shooting a doe in the wrong area!" His buddy said he had thought it was a buck and they surely could not leave it now to go to waste. They took the deer and dragged it out to the edge of the road where they stashed it in the ditch. The storyteller then goes to get his pickup. When he returned to the area where they had stashed the deer they unloaded their guns, put them in their cases. They then threw the deer in the back of the pickup and slammed the door on the pickup cap, jumped in to get out of the area as fast as they could.

He pulled out and headed out of the area, thinking all the time if they get caught there goes his hunting license, his gun, and a big fine! As they pulled over the top of the first hill, who is sitting in the middle of the road, but the game warden in his patrol car. The officer steps out and motions for them to stop as they come toward his car. The driver told me that his whole shirt and long underwear are water logged from the cold sweat he was in! They pull up to the officer and he says, "How are you guys doing?" As he starts to walk toward their pickup with the untagged, illegally shot deer in the back. All this time, our second hand culprit is sitting there watching his whole life pass before his eyes.

Just before the officer gets to the pickup, where he will be able to look into the back and see the deer laying there, they all hear a voice shout over his patrol car radio, "Get down here right away, there's blood all over the road down here!"

The officer turns around, jumps into his patrol car and takes off down the hill to the blood spot in the road made from the deer in the back of the pickup he just left. Well, you just don't catch them all.

A little while later this same party came by my booth with his buddy and said, "This is the clown that almost got me in serious trouble a few years ago!" I told him, "Your buddy feels a lot better now because he has carried this guilt around with him for years and confession is good for the soul." They both laughed and almost at the same time said, "You can bet we never did anything that stupid again."

Natural Blinds

As most people that hunt know there has been a debate going on for years about the use of hunting blinds. There are those that like to use them and there are those that feel that they should be outlawed. I personally think that a person should be able to hunt by any means they like if it does not adversely affect what they are hunting. I think there are too many people and special interest groups trying to get their way of doing things as the only legal way, but that is another story.
When this blind issue was being handled by the Exspurts they came up with the idea that they must be made of *natural* material. Now this could prove technically interesting.

For you see, these same people are always trying to get us to recycle items. If this is the case, I want to lay the following facts before you.

Eino had a real problem with the wording of *natural material* only. The rules that Teivo gave him a copy of read, "Any blind made of other then *natural material* must be removed from the woods each night after the day's hunt."

Now if we are going to be fair and impartial about this you have to take in all the facts, not only those you agree with. Lets start, wood comes from trees right? Trees grow out in the woods right? Then how can you say wood is not a *natural material?* So if you use anything made of wood you are really just returning it back to its roots, it's environment-friendly, right? Recycling right?

Then you must remember that plastic is a bi-product of oil; oil comes from decomposed trees and other vegetation right? So if you use any plastics this too is just being returned back to where it started from, right? We call this recycling.

Now Eino thinking back when he was attending school in Ontonagon, didn't they teach us that iron ore came from the ground. Therefore if nails and such are made out of this natural material found in the ground, iron ore, does not this mean....
Then Eino had another idea. If you are supposed to make your blinds of all natural material it only leaves a couple of possibilities. First, he thought of making a blind out of just sticks and brush.

Now we all know there is a lot of this lying around the woods so this should be no problem at all. Then he got thinking about all the work involved with collecting all these sticks and branches to make a blind. Then really how sturdy would a blind like this really be with all the snow on it? So he got an easier idea.

Why not just get some bales of straw and stack them in a square, leaving one side open to form a blind. There should be nothing to this, seeing all the bales are square and it would be just like using cement blocks to build something only larger. This idea showed promise.

While this idea was still forming in his mind back at his trailer, he picked up an outdoor paper and read where the DNR was now letting wolves loose out in the woods. Somehow when he read this while he was still thinking about building his deer blind out of sticks or straw, something kept eating away at the back of his mind.

What was it he had heard as a youth about building out of natural material, then something about the big, bad wolf coming along and wrecking it? But this tale must have been one of those old, last, generation stories.

So as Eino says, it is important to understand what the term *natural material* means and to believe in recycling or else you could get into trouble out there.

Dad could get you killed

Back during the good old days an officer spent a good many hours out in the woods after dark trying to catch shiners. It almost becomes like the war games we used to play when we were in the army.

On this evening we were working along Little Harbor Road, south of Thompson. We had received a few complaints about some night activity-taking place in an old apple orchard down in this area. We ran down into the area through some back trails without using our headlights so we could hide in the area of the orchard.

After sitting here for more than an hour we saw the glow of headlights coming through the woods into the orchard from the backside. We moved the patrol car and parked it just around a curve, over a little knoll. This way they could not see the car until the last minute and it blocked off the 2-track road the shiners were on.

We then walked a couple of hundred feet up the two-track in the orchard and ducked down behind some Lilac brush. As the pickup we were watching made its way to us we could see someone shining a hand-held spotlight, working the orchard looking for deer. We waited until they were right between us and turned on our flashlights, yelling, "Conservation Officer! Hold it right there!" The driver of the pickup just pushed the gas peddle to the floor trying to get out of the orchard onto Little Harbor Road to escape.

There was only one problem, no make that two problems!

The first problem was his boy was standing in the back of the pickup with a 30-06 rifle waiting for them to spotlight a deer. When dad floored the truck his son went flying backwards trying to catch his balance before he came sailing off over the tailgate of the truck.

The second problem was, just about the time the pickup picked up speed going over the knoll, it's headlights lite up the patrol car blocking the road! So dad had no choice but to slam on the brakes to keep from hitting the patrol car.

When he did this the son who was flying backwards for the tailgate one minute, quickly reversed his direction, now going forward once again, toward the front of the truck. That is until he smacked into the cab of the truck and slides off it onto the bed of the pickup. Needless to say it took all the desire to run right out of him.

Author with his to much coffee buck

Chapter 18

Conservation Officer's Stories

Upper Michigan Tales from a Game Warden's
Perspective

Exspurts Are Scary

Sometime back I attended a big outdoor show down in Grand Rapids, Michigan to try to peddle a few books. Needless to say, while you are there, you get to meet and talk to all kinds of people. Now, if you have read enough of the Fish Reports you would not have to be a rocket scientist to figure out what I think of Exspurts!

You know my beliefs will not allow me to believe in evolution, but just maybe, could it be? You can take a person that was never a real ball of fire from the first day they were hired, then they can become like a fungus that attaches itself to a tree, then they survive because of what or whom they are attached to. The next thing you know they have moved up a few steps in life, while still firmly attached to the tree, and the next thing you know they have evolved into an Exspurt!

Now there is also a short cut to becoming an Exspurt. But in either case the results are the same. It is called college! This is the person that the day they walk into a job they flat let everybody know they have arrived. Either form of an Exspurt can be deadly.

Well, before I get in any deeper, I have to ask you if you believe in spankings? If you don't, you are already on the wrong side of this deep, scientific, statement.

While down in Grand Rapids I had the chance to run into one of these retired Exspurts and if there is a danger from a normal Exspurt, really watch out for a retired Exspurt! This retired Exspurt made a statement that drives me right up a wall!

It goes like this, "The morale in the DNR is gone! With this governor we have now there is none! Nobody really cares if they even do their job with this governor we have!"

Now, the amazing thing with these Exspurts is that this gray- haired, old man, has been around through republican, through democrats, back into republicans and they have used the same statement to try and justify why they are either doing or not doing what they are supposed to be doing. I have to ask you, where else but in a protected government job could a party be making well more than $50,000 a year, with super benefits, and because somebody hurt their feelings or is not doing things the way they want them done, they sit and pout? Do you believe in spankings?

I guess as a taxpayer and also someone that knows the system I am getting a little tired of this whining. I wonder what would happen if an executive tried this in private industry and had this same attitude? How long do you think they would last?

Maybe I should tell you this so you will understand that I am not speaking out of turn. When I was still working, I took the exam for a promotion. I ended up having the highest score in the state for this job with a score of 98. But, when it came time for the promotions I soon found out that I was never to be offered one. When I questioned why I was passed over, I was told, "It's your religious belief." You see I am one of those old squares that if I had to be away from home I did not go out to party with the good old boys. Just because wifee was hundreds of miles away did the rules change? I usually brought along a few Louis L'Amour's western books, bought a pop and sat in my room to read in the evenings.

But the point is, did I still do my job until the day I retired? Yes. Let me tell you a story that may help make my point and explain how I feel about this type attitude.

There was this father that had a daughter that brought a report card home with a bad grade. When he questioned his daughter about it, she claimed the teacher was cruel and unfair. So dad told her come on and out to the car they went. They then went up to the high school into her classroom to see the teacher. The father, with his surprised daughter in tow, said to the teacher, "My daughter says you have not given her a fair grade on her report card and that you are being unfair to her, is this true?"

The teacher took out his grade book and showed the father where his daughter had not been doing all her homework. The grade was justified. Needless to say the daughter was now in deep trouble, but the point is she never expected her dad to do what he did, make her accountable for herself. She was asked, "Who do you think you are, if you don't do your homework, and keep up your part of what is required, that you should get a good grade?" He told me that this is the only time he ever had this type problem because he made his children accountable for what they did.

Now, I ask you why do adults blame someone else for their problems instead of realizing they and only they are accountable for their personal actions. But, then again, maybe if you are old and gray-headed you thought, this was true, but you have to remember we are in a new century now.

Hey! All you old people out there! Do you remember being taught, "People can change, things can change, but right and wrong never changes!" But, then again just maybe...

The times before Exspurts
Life with the old Timers and it was great

Well, if you are so young that you never had a chance to be around and work with the good old guys that made up the law division of the old Conservation Department you sure missed out.

Most of these guys had spent their tour of duty in the big war and had a whole different outlook on life than people do today. In fact, if you were one of those guys that flew in the big bombers you were extra special. But, if on top of this you were a tail or nose gunner you were something extra, extra special. Maybe this is why some of them were a little nuts to be around.

Of course you have to remember that back then radios were something to be used when and if you could ever make contact with someone. In fact, back then you drove your own car on patrol. When I first started out as a game warden, I drove my own 1961 Chevy while out on patrol.

One other thing that I found out to really be interesting is the number of older game wardens that did not even bother to wear their pistols while out on patrol. They just never felt they were needed with the type people Conservation Officers were dealing with most of the time back in those olden days.

I guess one of the first things I was to learn was that you had to earn your new uniforms. It seems that the man in charge of issuing uniforms felt that there was no way a lowly recruit should be issued new uniform parts. So you were issued parts from uniforms that the older officers had worn out and turned back in. I will say that this man was an excellent tailor and could even make old uniform parts fit a man with my build. I wore some of these hand-me-down uniforms for the first twenty years of my career before there was a change in the way things were issued.

But I'm not complaining because I still got to wear the uniform that so few people ever did. When I took the civil service test for Conservation Officer more than 3,500 people that took it and only about fifty passed it. Of these fifty the list was cut down to around thirty-eight that we were hired from. Life was great and I was right where I wanted to be.

It was nothing back then to have what we called group patrols. This was where a number of officers got together and went and worked an area for up to a week or more. A lot of times it was for opening day of waterfowl or deer season. You would not believe the stories and all the laughter that went around during these patrols.

I can remember an officer telling about the time he first went on one of these group patrols as a rookie officer. He said he wanted to be sure he did everything right and wanted to fit in. They got to the area where they would be camping. Things were set up and a little while later they realized they were missing something to use for a table.

Now you had to have a table! Where else could you play cards and this crew would never have survived if they could not have their card games, besides you did need something to cook and set the food on. They looked around and sure enough they found an object that would make a perfect table for all their needs. It was the new, young officers new suitcase.

So they set it up and for the rest of the time spent on the group patrol his new suitcase was both the kitchen and card table. Needless to say when he returned home the new suitcase was not the same one his wife had sent him off with.

One of the other things I was soon to learn was the interesting way some of these old timers looked at paperwork. They had their own interesting way of doing it.

There was one officer that lived in the county next to where I was assigned that always said this about his monthly reports. "All you have to do is go to the files, then go back five years, pull out one for the same month you need one for. Then all you do is change the date and make sure the names are right and it will fit right in." It sure sounded good to me seeing that it was a real bummer to have to type up a monthly report each month. So I got a better idea.

Dave, one of the guys I worked with, knew what a typewriter was for and could even use one. So he could hammer up a good monthly report in no time at all. I figured seeing we worked together so often I could handle this, too. So under his name on his monthly report I typed, "*I did the same things Dave did this month.*", and signed my name right under his.

This report took three days to get to the District Office. But only about three seconds to get back to me! Telling me that the system would not allow for me doing this. I had to do my own monthly report.

But the funny thing about these reports was the way some officers did them. There was and maybe still is the famous Monday morning report, so the wheels will have something to think about. I have heard officers that could give one of these Monday morning reports that would make you think they were supermen. The only thing was some of them never left their house all week long, but could they give a good report. I often wonder if the Monday morning report was truly supposed to be on what you had accomplished or actually was really on what you should have accomplished?

But some of these good report givers were soon filling the bill of being well on their way to becoming an Exspurt in Lansing.

....

Maybe this true tale is one that will give you an idea of just how things were back then. There was this party that spent about 99% of his time out violating. The other one percent he slept. We were always getting complaints about his activities, but he lived so far out in the woods he was hard to catch.

One night when working by myself, I happened to see him going up a dead end road. I waited for him to come out and stepped out in the road and told him to stop! He floored the car he was driving, heading right at me with it. I had to dive into the ditch to keep from getting hit.

A couple of days later my boss called me and told me to meet him at the office. When I got there, he was with a Lt. from the State Police. It seems that this party from a couple of nights before had turned me into the State Police saying I had shot at him. He even had a bullet hole in his car to prove it. Needless to say Lansing was in a panic! And I was surely worried about just what may come of this.

I told them I had not even pulled my pistol let alone fired a shot. Besides we all know a Yooper can't do two things at once and I was too busy diving in the ditch to get out of the way. Also, I'm not sure I could hit something as small as a car. The State Police had checked out the car and sure enough there was a bullet hole in the trunk. The only thing was, there was a bullet hole into the outer part of the trunk, but no sign of the bullet itself anywhere in the trunk or trunk lid. But this did not end the matter with Lansing, even if it did with everybody else.

So we had to meet at the county prosecutor's office to wait for a phone call from the law division chief in Lansing. We were sitting there talking when the phone rang and needless to say I had no idea what to expect seeing I was a new officer. The boss from Lansing got on the phone and talked to Jim, my boss, for a minute and then they put it on a speakerphone.

The boss asked just what had happened and Jim and the prosecutor told him about the complaint and what the State Police had found out. It finally all narrowed down to just what the local prosecutor thought about things and just what he would do about it.

Being new on the job I was not sure what to expect from this meeting.

The boss from Lansing asked the county prosecutor what he thought about what had taken place. You could tell he was worried and did not know what to expect either. But the prosecutor, who was one of the most respected in Michigan at the time, said, and I can still hear it in my mind today after all these years, "Well, George if it had been me out there I

<u>would </u>have shot the outlaw when he tried to run me over with his car!"

There was dead silence on the phone for a couple of seconds, and then the boss said Ok and hung up. That was the end of things and it never came up again.

J.A.W.'S Publication - Stories From a Game Warden

Sgt. John A. Walker
Author-Publisher
530 Alger Ave.
Manistique, MI 49854

Telephone 906-341-2082
Fax 906-341-2082
or 906-341-5914

Dear Friends,

I wish there was really somehow you could see my heart to know how thankfull I am for all the help you have been with my scholarship project from the sales of my books. Since my first book *A Deer Gets Revenge* came out the Lord has really blessed.

With the spring season here even in the north country things are really starting to pick up. My book orders have also picked right up. This past week I had to order the forth printing of *A Deer Gets Revenge* and a second printing of *Luck, Skill, Stupidity*. Without your help and all the others who have helped me out this would never have happened.

To date we have almost $20,000 in Certificates of Deposits for the scholarship fund at Bethel Baptist Church. I am trying to keep this as a base to increase through the interest from these Certificates until there is enough in the account to operate off the interest for years to come.

We have also been able to hand out over $7250.00 in scholarships to youth attending Christian Colleges since this project first began. If things go right this summer and the Lord continues to bless we will go over $10,000.00 given in scholarships in the next year. It is really hard to comprehend how this has happened, but with all your help we have been able to do it.

I wish you could read some of the letters I receive from the collage students about how thankful they are for this help. It is also amazing the letters I receive from all over the country from people that have purchased my books at the outlets around the state. For some reason after reading the books the people who bought them feel they have made a friend. I receive letters about their families and even get asked to write and encourage their children in their goals for life.

One of the most amazing things that I have been told over and over, by people who help me out, is how the Lord has also blessed their business for doing this. It is no secret that selling my books is really a favor to me to help with the scholarship fund. The few dollars most people make by doing this would really not change their income bracket for the IRS. But, it seems that when they were willing to help someone out with little or no earthly rewards, the Good Lord saw they were blessed for their effort.

Well thanks again for helping me out and may you have a great summer season.

Your Friend,

ORDER FORM: J.A.W.'S Publications
530 Alger Ave.
Manistique, MI 49854
(906) 341-2082

Name:_____

Address: _____

_____

A Deer Gets Revenge .... $10.00 Postpaid
From the Land Where BIG Fish Live .... $10.00 Postpaid
Luck, Skill, Stupidity .... $10.00 Postpaid
Humans are Nuts! .... $10.00 Postpaid

If a set of these 4 books are ordered from me I included a copy my out of print book
A Bucket of Bones free. Complete set of 5 books $40.00 postpaid

A Deer Gets Revenge ISBN 0-9639798-0-9
A Bucket of Bones ISBN 0-9639798-1-7
From the Land Where Big Fish Live ISBN 0-9639798-2-5
Some Call It Luck, Some Skill, But Just
Maybe Stupidity? (Can We Ever Really Tell) ISBN 0-9639798-3-3
Humans are Nuts! ISBN 0-9639798-4-1